ZANDRA RHODES

50 FABULOUS YEARS IN FASHION

Yale University Press, New Haven and London

pp. 2–3
Jasper Conran, Paul Smith, Stephen Jones, Zandra Rhodes,
Manolo Blahnik, Philip Treacy, Roland Mouret and Hussein
Chalayan as 'The Style Council'. British *Vogue*, December 2006.
Photo: Mario Testino © / Vogue © The Condé Nast Publications Ltd.

above
Zandra Rhodes in punk attire from the 1977/78
'Conceptual Chic' collections.
Photo: Eric Bowman.

CONTENTS

Zandra Rhodes, watercolour portrait by David Downton, 2017.

FOREWORD

Suzy Menkes

With shocking pink hair and dresses decorated, punk-style, with safety pins, Zandra Rhodes burst into a fashion era that was named for its raw energy – 'Swinging London'. Her dramatic shows in the 1970s were a template for fashion as theatre and entertainment. In an era when traditional cultural and social mores were only just being ousted, Zandra, with verve and energy, joined a youthful generation.

But behind the wild scenes and the torn seams, the designer was an exceptional creator, whose inventive prints followed the contours of the body in a unique way. Combining age-old techniques – from American Indian tribal patterns, through Japanese calligraphy, to Australian Aboriginal markings – Zandra was a mistress of modernity. Decades before the digital era, she studied at the Royal College of Art, London, and ultimately revolutionised print, producing effects that were entirely original. When Valentino resurrected these patterns 40 years on, in 2017, artistic director Pierpaolo Piccioli proved that Zandra Rhodes inventions were still relevant in the new millennium.

Other designers over the years have followed her distinctive concepts, including Gianni Versace's 1990s rendition of the safety-pin dress for actress Elizabeth Hurley. Meanwhile, Zandra herself was dressing the young Diana, Princess of Wales. A memorable dress was the feather-light pink chiffon gown with pearls like water drops, worn for a state visit by the Prince and Princess of Wales to Kyoto in 1986 (see p. 17).

In contrast, Zandra also made wild performance outfits for Brian May and Freddie Mercury, from the band Queen. These garments were recreated by Zandra for the 2018 Oscar-winning film *Bohemian Rhapsody* and worn by Rami Malek and Gwliym Lee, who played Mercury and May respectively. When the designer moved to California in order to be close to her partner Salah Hassanein, a former president at Warner Bros., Zandra was able to explore her skill in costume, bringing *The Magic Flute* to the San Diego Opera in 2001, followed by Georges Bizet's *The Pearl Fishers* in 2004 and Giuseppe Verdi's *Aida* at the Houston Grand Opera in 2007.

At the same time, she nurtured her British roots, founding the Fashion and Textile Museum in south London in 2003. It has hosted exhibitions from designers with a penchant for print – not least her own work. And for her knowledge and support, she was appointed first chancellor of the University for the Creative Arts, where her mother had once worked as a teacher in the former Medway College of Design. She is also, officially, Dame Zandra Rhodes – a formal tribute to a near-60-year career.

What is the secret of this long-term success? 'Unique' is a much-repeated word in the fashion lexicon, but Zandra Rhodes, with her imagination and invention, truly lives up to that description.

PREFACE

Iris Apfel

2019. What a wonderful time to be alive! The world is in chaos and the fashion industry even more chaotic.

'Life imitates art far more than art imitates life' – so wrote Oscar Wilde in his 1889 essay 'The Decay of Lying'. What a quote! True in today's world more than ever. This quote holds true within my own life and in that of the remarkable Zandra Rhodes.

Let's start this story from the beginning: born and raised in traditional England, Zandra built up quite the resilience to convention. With her bright pink coloured hair, her drawn-on eyebrows and her eccentric get-ups, she wandered her way right into the hearts of aspiring designers and adoring fans, and piqued the interest of some of the world's most prominent people. Her growing list of A-list celebrity clients included Elizabeth Taylor, Donna Summer, Diana Ross, Jacqueline Kennedy Onassis and Lauren Bacall. That's not to mention her impressive record with British royalty: Zandra has dressed Diana, Princess of Wales; Anne, Princess Royal; Princess Margaret, Countess of Snowdon; Princess Michael of Kent; and Sarah, Duchess of York.

My husband Carl and I founded Old World Weavers in 1950, so we were no strangers to fabrics. Zandra always says: 'When I first started, I was just a textile designer who couldn't find the right job.' I could understand a buyer's reaction when Zandra's wiggles, swirls, stars and 'button flowers' jumped off the page at you: Wow! Well, think about what those sorry suckers are thinking now! If anyone appreciates a bold woman with a bright personality, it's me. To make it in this world you must know how to follow your gut. There's no road map to style. Zandra's designs, like her bold and vibrant attire, knocked poised English society straight into the future!

The story of how I met Zandra starts about 14 years ago. Harold Koda, then curator-in-chief at the Anna Wintour Costume Center at New York's Metropolitan Museum of Art, asked me to do an exhibition of my collection of jewellery, accessories and clothes. The exhibition got a lot of attention, and piqued Zandra's interest in me. Fast forward about nine years: I was having dinner at a restaurant in Palm Beach, Florida, and a small group of people approached the table to share their compliments for my work. From this group peeked a five-foot-tall woman with bright blue eyeliner and a fuchsia bob; I recognised Zandra immediately. We shared our mutual admiration, which led to a post-Christmas get-together at my apartment nearby. Christmas decorations were in their full glory: choo-choo trains blazing, and green and red lights glimmering. Zandra, Carl and I sat for hours and must have shared about a million stories.

At the Museum of Art and Design's *LOOT: MAD About Jewelry* event in the spring of 2017, Zandra was the honorary chair. She was sporting one of her favourite necklaces with silver balls, and a gold spiked necklace underneath, both from India. Her dress was blue-and-black, one-shouldered chiffon, printed in her famous 'Knitted Circle' print, accessorised with her signature Andrew Logan brooches and bracelets. Her iconic get-up captivated the room. Zandra, her dear friends John Waters, Anna Sui, Daphne Guinness, Pat Cleveland and I had a wonderful evening together.

The one thing I admire most about Zandra is her unparalleled originality. Like myself, she has never thought about what others would think or say. The beauty of

Zandra is that she quite literally wears her emotions on her sleeves. She just does what feels right to her and wears whatever makes her feel happy.

Today's fashion is all about gauging the consumers – what's hot, what'll sell and what will make it on the runway. But designers who follow these rules are creating from someone else's imagination. Zandra, on the other hand, uses her own. In a world that tells you to sit down, shut up and fit in, Zandra was born to stand out.

Zandra Rhodes posing for her Swarovski jewellery poster in the 1980s.
Photo: Robyn Beeche.

INTRODUCTION

Dennis Nothdruft

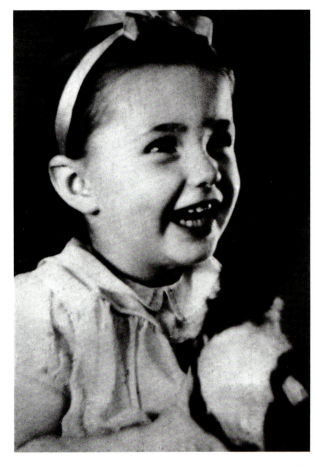

I loved designing textiles. I enjoyed the discipline of the prints, that they had to be cut and used economically, that I had to consider the measurements and repeats, that it was both technical and artistic at the same time, and directed towards an end product outside the pattern itself.[1]

To survive for 50 years in the push and pull of the fashion world is no mean feat. To remain an independent spirit, ploughing your distinctive furrow while the winds of change swirl about you, is an extraordinary one. Zandra Rhodes is one such extraordinary designer.

Her work has been defined by original printed textiles – defined by, but not limited to. Her vision, one that has found the most complete expression in her own appearance, encompasses everything around her. A fashion polymath, Rhodes has turned her hand to designing most things, including home furnishings, jewellery, footwear, handbags, eyewear, luggage, interiors, costumes and stage sets for opera, and furniture. What remains, the constant centre of Rhodes's oeuvre, is her hand: the line, the squiggle, the dash, the signature.

Her work in fashion, textiles and related fields of design has placed Rhodes at the centre of the fashion industry, while her own approaches and methods have the workings of an extended art project. It is this duality that makes Zandra Rhodes such an intriguing figure in the story of modern style.

BEGINNINGS

Zandra Lindsay Rhodes was born in Chatham, Kent, in the southeast of England. Her mother Beatrice – an exotic presence whom Rhodes often cites – had worked as a fitter at the fashion house of Worth and subsequently taught fashion. Rhodes's own prodigious talent for art was evident early on. Surviving sketchbooks for her school art projects show a keen eye for observation, a skill that would inform her work as a professional designer.

Rhodes's initial thought was to be an illustrator; this only changed after studying with the influential textile designer Barbara Brown, whose work for Heal's Fabrics was some of the most well known of the late 1950s and early 1960s. This experience changed the course of Rhodes's future career plans; it was then that she decided to study textile design. With Brown's prompting, Rhodes applied to the Royal College of Art (RCA) in London, at that time the most important art school in the country.

In the years immediately following the Second World War, art schools in Britain provided an opportunity for people from a diverse range of backgrounds to study art and design. The influx of students, many of whom had served in or lived through the war, was the beginning of a flowering of talent in these areas. Upon graduation, these artists and designers revitalised the post-war cultural

above
Photograph of Zandra Rhodes as a child in the 1940s.
below
Page from Rhodes's sketchbook from Medway College of Art, showing drawings of hands.

1   Anne Knight and Zandra Rhodes, *The Art of Zandra Rhodes*, London: Jonathan Cape, 1984, p. 11.

landscape; by the 1960s, the country was influencing popular culture around the globe. The RCA was at the forefront of this groundswell of talent. The fashion department, under the direction of Madge Garland and then Janey Ironside, produced a group of fashion designers that would change the course of fashion at home and abroad for decades.

AT THE CENTRE: ROYAL COLLEGE OF ART

The RCA in the 1960s was the epicentre of contemporary art and design in Britain. The master's-only programmes took the best and the brightest of the country's young talent. What made it special was the mix: students from across disciplines would interact and exchange ideas. During the years when Rhodes attended, the RCA was the fulcrum of Pop Art, and the presence of students like David Hockney (who was already gaining a following) and Derek Boshier would, in turn, influence her work.

Rhodes attended the RCA from 1962 to 1965, the three-year course providing the designer with numerous opportunities to explore her chosen medium of printed textiles. One of the keys to Rhodes's designs has been her knowledge of the physical processes involved in designing and printing silk-screened textiles. What appears to flow so effortlessly from the designer is in reality a carefully thought-out print – the result of months of cutting apart and readjusting the pattern to get the exact effect desired. It was in her second year that Rhodes chose to specialise in dress fabrics; the trend at the time was for furnishing fabrics. This choice, to create printed textiles to be worn rather than hung or used as upholstery, would lead the designer to her most innovative ideas.

Rhodes began to explore the relationship of printed fabric to the body underneath it, discovering that the form of the human figure underneath the textile provides a constantly changing 'landscape' that the print interacts with and defines anew. By creating paper patterns that she would pin and wrap around her own figure, studying the effect in mirrors to create a distance between the designer and the print, Rhodes would explore the potential of a printed material to shape the garment itself. Cutting into fabric was more than a case of laying out a dress pattern for Rhodes – judicious use of print would guide the cutting of the fabric and the structure of the garment. What may not seem particularly radical today was an innovative approach then.

Her time at the RCA continues to define Rhodes as a designer and artist. The interaction with other artists and designers would provide her with an interdisciplinary approach that has allowed her to blur the boundaries of textile design, painting, performance and fashion throughout her working life.

POP GOES THE TEXTILE

My work was becoming more and more figurative – reflecting the Pop world about me, becoming less and less abstract.[2]

Rhodes's textile designs are a reflection of both her interests and her experiences. Her early designs, from the art school days

above
Page from Rhodes's sketchbook from Medway College of Art, showing studies of faces.
below
Rhodes's pen and ink sketch of the wood yards in Strood, Kent, in the late 1950s.

2   Ibid., p. 20.

through the 1970s, are an exploration of the popular culture around her. For some design historians, Rhodes's printed textiles are another medium for Pop Art, the defining art movement of the 1960s. Pop Art provided a new visual language and aesthetic for artists and designers of the era. Pop's appropriation of popular culture and its attendant images would become a stylistic trope, a strategy of repetition for those working across a range of media. Rhodes's magpie aesthetic gathers together light bulbs from the Blackpool Illuminations, comic strips, neon lights, the Thunderbirds, sequins, explosions, stars and teddy bears in the earliest prints.

The hand-drawn and -painted quality of the silk-screen prints would become a defining feature of her work at this stage. An almost ad hoc feel in the earliest prints belies the time and effort involved in their creation. A notable example is the 'Medals' group – the collection of textiles the designer produced for her graduation collection.

THE HOUSE OF ZANDRA RHODES: 1969

I now had to learn to take these prints into the world of fashion. I had never been trained as a fashion designer, but I did not think it could be such a mystery. I had only to find out how to start.[3]

Rhodes began her career selling textiles directly to fashion designers. The most successful of these were her works for Marion Foale and Sally Tuffin, fellow alumni of the RCA who had established a successful fashion label in 1962. Foale and Tuffin produced youthful, easy-to-wear dresses, trousers and suits for the modern young woman. Their work projected a certain insouciance, almost rebelliousness – an image promoted by the two designers themselves. Foale and Tuffin referred to themselves, on more than one occasion, as 'bolshy'.[4]

Following this, Rhodes soon joined forces with fashion designer Sylvia Ayton, a classmate of Foale and Tuffin's at the RCA. Together, Ayton and Rhodes launched the Fulham Road Clothes Shop, with clothing designed by Ayton, made up in textiles designed by Rhodes. Though short-lived – the shop was open for a year only – the experience convinced Rhodes to continue with her concept of printed textiles as the defining element of a garment, rather than an afterthought. The partnership ended in 1968, and by 1969 Rhodes was designing under her own label.

Rhodes chose to design her garments as well as the textiles, a bold move for someone without any training in fashion design. It was a constant refrain in those early days – 'once a textile designer, always a textile designer' – and one that Rhodes's success has refuted time and again.

THE FIRST COLLECTIONS

To create her very first collection as the house of Zandra Rhodes, the designer turned, once again, to the environment around her.

top
Rhodes's 'Lightbulb' textile print design on paper, 1967.
middle
Rhodes's 'Top Brass' textile print design on cotton sateen produced as a furnishing fabric for Heal's and displayed in her diploma show at the RCA in 1964.
bottom
Rhodes's 'Chevron Shawl' textile print design on calico, 1970.

3 Ibid., p. 26.
4 Author interview with Zandra Rhodes, October 2018.

New currents were beginning to move through contemporary culture, as the youthful and forward-looking ideals of the 1960s gave way to a longing for the past and simpler times. This past may have been a fantasy rather than a reality, but it would inform much of the cultural movement of the 1970s, which favoured a more eclectic and varied approach to style.

These currents were picked up by Rhodes, who turned to traditional folk costumes, as documented in the Victorian ethnographer Max Tilke's colour drawings, for shapes and construction details. These simplified forms, clearly laid out in Tilke's illustrations, provided a starting point for Rhodes's fantasies. The designer exaggerated sleeves, added gathers and volume, and put seams on the outside of her garments; the use of printed fabrics with designs by Rhodes only added to the creations.

Rhodes began drawing the knitted bedcovers and embroidered shawls in London's Victoria and Albert Museum. Knitting instruction books, with their carefully drawn diagrams of stitches and loops, became another element of the 'Knitted Circle' collection of 1969. The prints were huge circles of drawn chain stitches and knitted flowers – these the designer transformed into kaftans and dresses, quite unlike anything anyone had seen. We also find here the use of silk chiffon, soon to become the quintessential material for a Zandra Rhodes creation.

With the 'Chevron Shawl' and 'Indian Feathers' collections of the following year, Rhodes introduced another feature of her work – cutting around a printed pattern to create shape, detail and structure. The 'Chevron Shawl' print of 1970 was inspired by Victorian shawls, particularly the fringed edging. Rhodes draws the fringe and tassels into the print; she then cuts around the drawn tassels to create the illusion of fringing. Constructed in soft chiffon or on stiff calico, these 'essences' of fringed tassels define the shape of the garment itself.

The seminal 'Indian Feathers' prints, which Rhodes created following a trip to New York, featured a similar technique. The designer drew the feathers that feature on traditional American Indian costume, including the porcupine-quill stitches that hold them in place. These initial drawings were translated, stitches and all, to a series of textile prints. The borders, edges and joins on the resulting garments were the printed feathers, cut around and hand rolled. This circularity – a drawing of a feather embellishment cut and sewn to create the illusion of a feather embellishment – was typical of Rhodes's approach.

THE HIGH STYLE OF THE 1970s

In 1976, the journalist Peter York published an article in *Harpers & Queen*. This article, entitled 'Them', identified a group of artists, designers and personalities who defined, for York, the high style of the 1970s.[5] As the author, with fellow journalist Ann Barr, of the original article defining the 'Sloane Ranger', York was perfectly placed as a lifestyle and cultural commentator to describe this

5   Peter York, *Style Wars*, London: Sidgwick and Jackson, 1980, p. 120.

above
Carolina Herrera wearing her favourite dress from the Zandra Rhodes 1972 'The Lily' collection, sitting with daughter, Carolina. *Harper's Bazaar*, July 1974.
Photo: Maria von Matthiessen.
below
Donna Summer on her 'Once Upon a Time' album cover in 1977, wearing a Zandra Rhodes silk chiffon evening gown from the 1972 'The Lily' collection (see p. 35).
Photo: Francesco Scavullo.

new movement. Included in his loosely connected international network was Zandra Rhodes, the dress designer of choice for the high-fashion, ultra-stylish group.

By the time York had written this particular article, perhaps with tongue slightly in cheek, Rhodes had become a critical and commercial success as a fashion designer. Her distinctive style, both on the catwalk and in her own personal expression of self, had caught the attention of the international fashion press and buyers on both sides of the Atlantic. The designer's brand of avant-garde femininity struck a chord with women, both famous and not. Even the controversial 'Conceptual Chic' collection of 1977/78, Rhodes's riff on the punk movement, provided a beautiful alternative to rips, chains and safety pins.

DESIGN METHODS

Rhodes developed in the beginning of her career a set of working strategies that she still practises today. These methods would establish the designer as an emergent postmodernist in the late 1960s and early 1970s, and, while her work is less overtly retro than that of other designers of the time, these elements and her interdisciplinary interactions with friends and artists Andrew Logan and Duggie Fields place her career in the context of contemporary art movements. Within Rhodes's work is a historicist theme, one in which references are selected – Tudor clothing, American Indian embellishments – then segregated from their original context and mixed with other references to create new and original forms.

Rhodes's process always begins in the same way: detailed observational drawing in her sketchbook. This may be a drawing of a landscape or building, an object on display in a museum or gallery, or an image in a book or magazine. Indeed, any object, view or image has the potential to be translated into a drawing by the designer. These drawings in turn become the basis for a textile print design first, and then a dress, garment or look. Throughout the drawing and design process, Rhodes is continually filtering the work, forming links and blending incongruous elements. This method works to create a visual bricolage, whereby Rhodes's drawn images of things, rather than the things themselves, become grist for the creative mill. It is a method of working that has changed little since her days at the RCA, with merely a shifting of reference from the present-day culture to the past and back again. The allusions and quotes referenced by the designer are in a constant state of flux; some are discernible and others are not.

THE BIGGEST SHOWS

By the 1980s, Rhodes was producing fashion spectacles – the culmination of London's fashion week. Her catwalks featured elaborate choreography, sets – often by Andrew Logan – dancers, special effects and the most exotic hair, make-up and accessories. These fashion shows were legendary: the 'Fables of the Sea' show in 1984 featured a Poseidon character rising up from below the stage.

above
'Poseidon', character design by Zandra Rhodes, backstage at the Spring/Summer 1984 'Fables of the Sea' fashion show. Mask and trident: Andrew Logan.
Photo: Robyn Beeche.
below
The Fashion and Textile Museum in Bermondsey, London before its opening.
Photo: Patrick Anderson.

Increasingly, over the course of that decade, Rhodes became known for her party dresses: extravagant, often with full tulle and net skirts, heavily beaded bodices or large ruffled collars and full sleeves, and all featuring a print by Rhodes. These confections reached their apogee with dresses designed for clients such as 'Bubbles' (Patricia Harmsworth, Viscountess Rothermere).

Rhodes's growing international reputation saw the designer crossing the United States for a series of seasonal trunk shows. These exercises in selling featured the designer's latest collections, and offered clients a chance to receive advice and input from Rhodes herself. Rhodes was also invited to India in 1987 to design and produce a collection of saris and salwar kameezes. These garments were presented to an Indian audience in equally spectacular runway shows and included novelties such as panniers under saris, or top hats and walking sticks worn with saris, as well as the famous 'Holey Sari', which had embroidered holes through which the wearer could put her arm or face (see p. 127). India had never seen anything quite like it; the collections were initially offered to Indian customers only.

Working in India offered the designer the opportunity to design fully beaded dresses and tunics and trousers; these would be designed, produced in India by specialist artisans, and sold through the 1980s and into the 90s. This is another example of the reach of Rhodes's design career.

NEW CHALLENGES AND NEW HORIZONS

Throughout the 1990s, Rhodes continued to design collections; while the fashions of that decade embraced a minimalist or deconstructed aesthetic, the designer remained true to her vision. A sobering recession impacted the fashion industry around the world, and Rhodes was just one of many designers to re-evaluate and reposition their label. Her work of this period explored a variety of techniques: hand-painting, devoré fabrics, a revisited cutting and slashing.

Alongside producing collections, Rhodes undertook the biggest project of her career: the founding of the Fashion and Textile Museum in London. While the museum would not officially open until 2003, the project was underway by the mid-1990s. What originally began as a celebration of British design – particularly textile design, which Rhodes felt was under-represented in the industry – soon grew to take an international view. The championing of contemporary textiles and clothing in a gallery context would prove prescient, as the study of fashion and its attendant disciplines has become a subject of major exhibitions around the world.

Through it all, Rhodes's love of the printed pattern has continued – a sustaining thread from which hangs 50 years of fabulous.

Contemporary photograph of Zandra Rhodes.
Photo: Simon Emmett.

From the first collection in 1969, Zandra Rhodes's innovative use of printed fabrics was pivotal. A variety of materials – calico, satin, rayon jersey, felt and chiffon – highlighted Zandra's experimental spirit during these years. In 1977, Rhodes created the 'Conceptual Chic' collection, which lasted two seasons and featured couture garments inspired by street-style punk. Her revolutionary use of strategically placed holes ornamented with beaded safety pins, blue-mauve overlocking and sink chains named her for evermore the 'Princess of Punk'.

Oxana and Myroslava Prystay wearing Zandra Rhodes silk chiffon kaftans from the 1969 'Knitted Circle' collection. British *Vogue*, December 1969.
Photo: David Bailey / Vogue © The Condé Nast Publications Ltd.

1969–1979

this page
1969, 'Knitted Circle' collection.
Silk chiffon kaftan printed with
'Knitted Circle' design, style Z7.
opposite
Natalie Wood in a silk chiffon
kaftan with hood from the 1969
'Knitted Circle' collection.
American *Vogue*, January 1970.
Photo: Gianni Penati / Vogue ©
The Condé Nast Publications Ltd.

opposite
Natalie Wood in a yellow printed
wool felt coat from the 1969
'Knitted Circle' collection.
American *Vogue*, January 1970.
Photo: Gianni Penati / Vogue ©
The Condé Nast Publications Ltd.
this page
1969, 'Knitted Circle' collection.
Wool felt coat printed with 'Knitted
Circle' and 'Diamonds and Roses'
designs, style Z23.

1969–1979

this page and opposite (detail)
Spring/Summer 1970, 'Ukraine
and Chevron Shawl' collection.
Quilted cotton calico coat printed
with 'Chevron Shawl' design,
style 70/23. Kindly donated by
Evangeline Bruce.

Maudie James in a silk chiffon kaftan-style 'Chevron Shawl' jacket.
British *Vogue*, April 1970.
Photo: Henry Clarke / Vogue © The Condé Nast Publications Ltd.

Spring/Summer 1970, 'Ukraine and Chevron Shawl' collection. Silk chiffon evening ensemble with hand-rolled edges, with feathers on the tips, printed with 'Chevron Shawl' design, styles 70/4 (top) and 70/6 (skirt).

Spring/Summer 1970, 'Ukraine and Chevron Shawl' collection. Full-length silk chiffon evening dress with tiny satin bodice, printed with 'Giant Snail Flower' design, style 70/11.

Moyra Swan in a silk chiffon evening dress from the 'Ukraine and Chevron Shawl' collection. British *Vogue*, June 1970. Photo: David Bailey / Vogue © The Condé Nast Publications Ltd.

Ann Schaufuss in a quilted rayon satin coat from the Autumn/Winter
1971 'Paris, Frills and Button Flowers' collection. British *Vogue*,
October 1971.
Photo: Clive Arrowsmith / Vogue © The Condé Nast Publications Ltd.

Autumn/Winter 1971, 'Paris, Frills and Button Flowers' collection. Quilted rayon satin knee-length coat, printed with 'Button Flower' and 'Frilly Flower' designs, style 71/27.

this page
Autumn/Winter 1971, 'Paris, Frills
and Button Flowers' collection.
Wool felt coat with seams on
the outside and 'Button Flower'
printed satin accents, style 71/19.
opposite
'Greta' wearing a wool felt 'Button
Flower' coat from the 1971
'Paris, Frills and Button Flowers'
collection.
Photo: Bishin Jumonji.

opposite
Jane Goddard in a silk chiffon
evening gown from the 1972
'The Lily' collection. British
Vogue, April 1974.
Photo: David Bailey / Vogue ©
The Condé Nast Publications Ltd.
this page
Autumn/Winter 1972, 'The Lily'
collection. Silk chiffon evening
gown worn with satin sash, printed
with 'Field of Lilies' and 'Reverse
Lily' designs, style 73/44.

1969–1979

ZANDRA RHODES: 50 FABULOUS YEARS IN FASHION

pp. 38–39
Models wearing evening gowns from the 1974 'Ayers Rock'
collection and the 1976 'Cactus and Cowboy' collection,
British *Vogue*, April 1976.
Photo: Barry Lategan / Vogue © The Condé Nast Publications Ltd.

opposite
Spring/Summer 1976, 'Cactus and Cowboy' collection. Ultrasuede
top and matching trousers/chaps printed with 'Spinifix Border'
design, styles 76/U101 (top) and 76/U110 (trousers).

this page
Ultrasuede top and skirt from the 1976 'Cactus and Cowboy' collection.
Photo: Norman Eales.

Spring/Summer 1976, 'Cactus and Cowboy' collection. Ultrasuede
sleeveless jacket and matching knee-length skirt printed with 'Spinifix
Border' and 'Spinifix Square' designs, style 76/U109 (skirt).

Sue Purdy in an ultrasuede top and trousers worn with satin blouse
with pleated collar from the 1976 'Cactus and Cowboy' collection.
Photo: Barry Lategan.

Autumn/Winter 1976–78, 'Mexican' collections. Silk chiffon evening dress worn with a satin sash printed with 'Mexican Turnaround' design, style 77/10.

this page, right
Autumn/Winter 1976–78, 'Mexican' collections. Silk chiffon evening ensemble printed with 'Mexican Sombrero' design, style 76/26.

opposite
Models in evening gowns from the 1976–78 'Mexican' collections. Photo: Clive Arrowsmith.

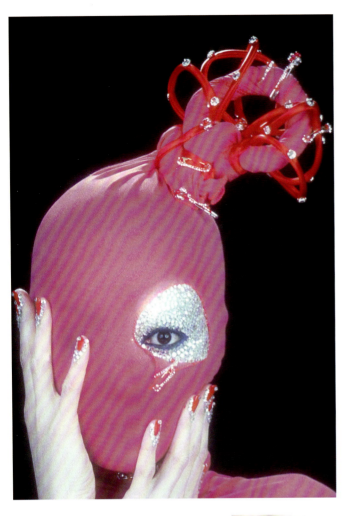

opposite, top left
Pink embroidered punk mask.
Make-up: Richard Sharah.
Photo: Grant Mudford.

opposite, top right and below
Details of garments from the
Spring/Summer 1977/78
'Conceptual Chic' collections,
including strategically placed
holes ornamented with beaded
safety pins, blue satin accents
and topstitching, a satin bodice
and sink chains.

this page
Spring/Summer 1977/78,
'Conceptual Chic' collections.
Full-length jersey dress with
red satin ribbon appliqué and
decorative holes ornamented with
beads and beaded safety pins,
worn with a wide black satin sash
with black jersey attached with
ornamented safety pins and sink
chains, styles 77/35 and 77/15.

Polly Eltes and Louise de Teliga in punk ensembles from the
1977/78 'Conceptual Chic' collections. Make-up: Richard Sharah.
Photo: Clive Arrowsmith.

ZANDRA RHODES IN AMERICA: REFLECTIONS ON A REFLECTOR

Marylou Luther

In Cambridge, Nebraska, population 1,063, there is a Zandra Rhodes Memorial Bedroom. I know. It's my bedroom. In my home there. On the wall in that bedroom are four Rhodes illustrations, one each from 1975, 1976, 1977 and 1982. Each measures 66 × 58 cm. Two feature Zandra as the model. So why, in my 64 years of covering fashion and design (yes, there's a difference), with interviews and book forewords on designers including Rudi Gernreich, Pierre Cardin, Thierry Mugler, Sonia Rykiel, Edith Head, Geoffrey Beene, Gianni Versace, Norman Norell, Halston, Alexander McQueen, John Galliano and Rick Owens – to name a few – would I want to go to sleep looking at Zandra Rhodes?

Answer: because Zandra not only creates clothes – clothes that have been copied or 'interpreted' by some of the most important designers in the world – Zandra creates art: wearable art. When I asked if she wanted to reveal some of the names of those who have designed 'homages' in her name, she began by saying how really honoured she was that so many important designers thought her work was homage-able. Then she showed me some very convincing sets of originals and copies. Then she told me the story of why she is reluctant to pursue the subject. 'I once called in a copyright lawyer, as I even had friends phoning to congratulate me on someone else's copy. All I ended up with was a bill for $2,000.'

Zandra is also one of the very few designers whose work reflects the times. (I digress here to say that the big reason fashion interests me is that it is one of the few art forms – music and movies included – that reflects a time, a movement, a 'moment' that merits a place in history.) Zandra's place was first established when she studied textile design at London's Royal College of Art. As she told me during one of my first trips to her studio in London, 'I could not find a job in textile design – no one could understand my work or "get it" – so I started creating apparel designs to show how the prints were practical and show how they were meant to be.' Here's how they were meant to be, in her own words:

> Textile prints are my main forte, and it constantly amazes me how the print can control the whole look and shape of a garment. I suppose I'm the forerunner of the digital print revolution, as prints have always controlled the look of my garments before other designers could work out how to do this. My clothes are engineered to accommodate the placement of the prints, rather than cut from continuous, repetitive yardage.

Zandra is famous for translating her travels from original sketchbook drawings into fabric prints, Zandra-ising everything from the Great Wall of China and Uluru/Ayers Rock in the Australian Outback to 'Vegas Vic', the neon waving cowboy on Fremont Street, Las Vegas.

One of the biggest fashion movements in history, the punk upheaval of the 1970s, inspired Zandra's first big international apotheosis. To set the scene: in their heyday on the King's Road, London, the punks were dubbed everything from neo-Fascist to alienated teenagers who worshipped the Sex Pistols and simply wanted to shock the establishment through the violence of their clothes and make-up. The young seditionaries connected their pierced nostrils to their pierced ears via old-fashioned electric light-pulls. They wore Mohawk hairdos, necklaces of paper clips and safety pins, and covered their bodies in recycled plastic bags. Zandra was the first designer to bring their street culture to the runway, in her 'Conceptual Chic' collections of 1977/78, elevating the holes and safety pins of punkdom to luxury fashion and thereby, arguably, becoming the first major designer to pioneer the street as a centre of fashion. (Yes, Vivienne Westwood did punk, but she didn't elevate the look to the heights of haute.) Designs from that collection are now at the Victoria and Albert Museum, London; The Metropolitan Museum of Art, New York; the Museums Victoria in Australia; and the designer's own Fashion and Textile Museum on Bermondsey Street, London.

On the subject of elevating looks, consider Zandra's own look. This daughter of a Paris fashion house fitter and teacher at Medway College of Design (this institution now part of the University for the Creative Arts) transformed herself, becoming the most instantly identifiable designer/celebrity of her time. When she first came to Los Angeles in the early 1970s, her hair was bright green with feathers at the end. Since then, her hair colour has ranged from pink to red to blue and orange – and shades thereof. Others would dye for her instant recognisability. As Zandra told me when we first met, in 1969:

> I decided that I must be an extension of my designs. I used myself as a canvas with no compromises: experimenting with my image, using cosmetics and my hair to create an impact. I have always been very extreme in my appearance, from sticking feathers with eyelash glue on the ends of my dyed green hair, to embroidering and patching jeans quite outrageously, to using blue make-up. I was inspired by a blue[-skinned] Indian god for my photograph on my India-inspired poster of 1982 [for 'The Indian' collection].

It was on Zandra's first LA trip in 1973 that I, as fashion editor of the *Los Angeles Times*, took her to meet the legendary Edith Head, winner of the most ever Academy Awards for costume design. With those eight Oscars at the ready, Edith wowed Zandra by showing her the guest house, with a sign reading 'Elizabeth Taylor Slept Here' at the front door, explaining that the actress loved staying with her instead of at the nearby Beverly Hills Hotel or the Beverly Wilshire Hotel because it freed her from the ever-vigilant paparazzi. In her travels across the US, doing shows for Neiman Marcus and Saks Fifth Avenue department stores, as well as her own shows

above, top to bottom

Blondie's Debbie Harry wearing a Zandra Rhodes punk gown from the 1977/78 'Conceptual Chic' collections. Photo: Sheila Rock ©. Jacqueline Kennedy Onassis wearing a one-shouldered Zandra Rhodes silk chiffon evening gown from the 1974 'Ayers Rock' collection to an event in 1976. Photo: Ron Galella.

above, top to bottom

Elizabeth Taylor wearing Zandra Rhodes and watching the fireworks with Malcolm Forbes in Balleroy, France in June 1988. Photo: Alexis Duclos. Zandra Rhodes with her early signature look of green hair with feathers on the ends, standing in Hyde Park in the 1960s. Photo: Stan Woodward.

in London, Zandra and her designs attracted clients that included Jacqueline Kennedy Onassis and her sister Lee Radziwill, Diana, Princess of Wales, Elizabeth Taylor, Bianca Jagger, Kylie Minogue, Paris Hilton, Isabella Blow, Debbie Harry, Lauren Bacall, Sarah Jessica Parker, Mica Ertegun, Evangeline Bruce, and, in 2017/18, through a set of print designs revived at Valentino, Meryl Streep, Frances McDormand, Anna Wintour and Keira Knightley. Zandra attracted me by way of her willingness to disrupt the status quo.

Once, when she invited me to her home for dinner, I walked up the stairs to be greeted by a great big bathtub. I saw it as a work of art – modern art. She told me she had just moved and that the only place to put it until the plumber came was at the top of the stairs. (Yes, her honesty is beguiling.)

Over the years, I have collected Zandra quotes. Here are some of my favourites:

On fantasy: 'When I start making a dress it might be fantasy, but by the time I've finished, it looks like reality – at least to me.'

On individuality: 'To make it in fashion you must be persistent in the pursuit of your individuality.'

On length: 'I don't think what length a dress should be. I try it on – I try everything on myself – and just let it happen.'

On success: 'Do not take success for granted. Hard work and originality get one there, but staying there is just as hard work. You can trip up any time.'

On aspiring designers: 'You can have anything you want in life but never when you want it. It's just like Alice in Wonderland – there are all the bottles on the shelves labelled "I want to be a famous designer." Just work hard, reach up and take them down and swallow them. But you can't then regurgitate. You must make it work.'

Zandra made it work. Among her many honours are her appointment as a Commander of the Order of the British Empire in 1997, her honorary doctorates from universities in both the UK and the US, and her damehood, bestowed by Princess Anne in 2015. Her designs have appeared at the Parsons School of Art and Design, New York; the Art Institute of Chicago; The Metropolitan Museum of Art, New York; the Smithsonian Institution, Washington, D.C.; the Victoria and Albert Museum, London; Texas Gallery, Houston; the Museum of Applied Arts & Sciences, Sydney; and the Museum of Contemporary Art San Diego, California.

Zandra is larger than life. A fashion eminence. A revolutionary. A true original. A reflector. A friend.

Cher wearing a Zandra Rhodes silk chiffon dress from the 1970
'Ukraine and Chevron Shawl' collection. American *Vogue*, October 1970.
Photo: Charles Tracy / Vogue © The Condé Nast Publications Ltd.

Freddie Mercury wearing a Zandra Rhodes white
pleated top in the *Queen II* concert tour, 1974.
Photo: Mick Rock © 1974, 2019.

ZANDRA RHODES
AS AN INSPIRATIONAL ICON

Anna Sui

When Zandra Rhodes asked me to write about my memories of attending her legendary 1974 'Circle in the Square' fashion show, I began thinking about how different it was back then, and how we got information before the era of internet and cellphones. All discoveries had to be made through the incredible journalists, newspapers and magazines of the time. I was totally obsessed – I combed through these publications daily to get glimpses into the world of fashion.

This led me to encounter a piece Priscilla Tucker had written about Zandra's upcoming show in her *New York Magazine* 'Best Bets' column. The headline was 'Getting the Rhodes on the Show'. She reported that Bianca Jagger was '99 per cent' sure to be modelling, and it was definitely 100 per cent confirmed that Orson Welles's daughter, Beatrice, would appear. The fashionable hairdresser Leonard of Mayfair was flying in from London to do the hair, 'in whatever colours'. Tickets for the 24 April extravaganza cost $35!

Zandra had had her first staged show in the UK two years earlier, at the Roundhouse in north London. The most legendary models of the time were featured: Donna Jordan, Cathee Dahmen, Susan Moncur, Caterine Milinaire, Pat Cleveland and Renate Zatsch. A photograph of Anjelica Huston by Clive Arrowsmith appeared on the poster. Bianca Jagger was in the audience. The show began at midnight, and David Bailey and Penelope Tree threw the after-party. Everyone was so impressed with its success that producer Gary Smith and his wife, the interior designer Maxine Smith, decided to bring the show to New York!

My friend Ruth Tishman and I went to the box office and bought tickets. It would be the first full-on fashion event I ever went to. I invited photographer Steven Meisel, and Ruth brought Paul Gearity. Paul designed clothes for Alice Cooper and Mick Jagger, and Ruth was wearing a crocheted dress he had made – a collage of granny doilies, à la The Cockettes' Richard 'Scrumbly' Koldewyn! I would wear my Zandra Rhodes cream silk jersey dress with 'Button Flower' trapunto appliqués and contrast-stitch lettuce edging, which I bought on sale at Henri Bendel. Over it, I wore my mom's cashmere, dolman-sleeve coat, which she had bought in Paris.

At this time, Zandra Rhodes was my ultimate designer idol. Her clothes were like a total dream. She was the first person I knew to have brightly coloured dyed hair. In May 1973, when Anne, Princess Royal, chose one of Zandra's lace 'The Shell' collection princess dresses for her official engagement photograph with Captain Mark Phillips, it established Zandra for evermore as a quintessential British designer.

above, top to bottom
Cathee Dahmen and Jacques Ross as the bride and groom finale at Rhodes's first major London fashion show, 'Midnight at the Roundhouse', in 1972. Photo: Clive Boursnell. Finale of 'Midnight at the Roundhouse' in 1972 with Donna Jordan, Cathee Dahmen, Susan Moncur, Caterine Milinaire, Pat Cleveland, Renate Zatsch and Zandra Rhodes. Photo: Clive Boursnell.

opposite
Anne, Princess Royal, wearing an embroidered net gown printed with 'Seashell' design for the announcement of her engagement to Captain Mark Phillips in 1973. Photo: Norman Parkinson.

ZANDRA RHODES: 50 FABULOUS YEARS IN FASHION

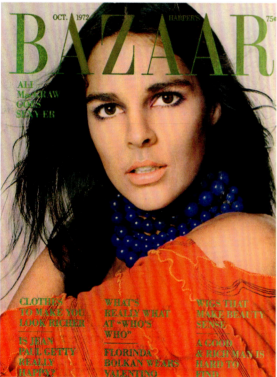

Years before the show, I searched for everything I could find out about Zandra. I clipped and collected photographs and articles. In January 1970, I remember a feature in American *Vogue* that showed Natalie Wood wearing Zandra's famous peaked-lapel circle coat in yellow wool felt, screen-printed on the circular yoke and skirt with the red-and-black 'Diamonds and Roses' pattern, in a repeat that made up a sort of plaid effect (as photographed by Gianni Penati, see p. 22). Natalie's second outfit was a hooded kaftan in Zandra's 'Knitted Circle' print, in shades of aqua and pink (see p. 21). Another favourite series of Gianni Penati images, also published in *Vogue* in that year, shows Zandra's dresses on Karen Graham. The floaty 'Snail Flower' print dress (a variation on the 'Squiggle' theme), tipped with feathers and curling ribbons that echoed Graham's ringlet hair, perfectly captured the exuberance and romanticism of Zandra's spirit.

She dressed the rock stars, too, like Marc Bolan and Freddie Mercury. In an issue of *Interview* magazine from 1970, Zandra described a draped shirt she had just made for Bolan: 'Very low, all bits of frilly jersey attached to it, yellow edged with turquoise and machined in red thread. It sort of aggravates the eye.'

I also loved the June 1970 issue of American *Vogue*, featuring photos of Caterine Milinaire veiled in one of Zandra's squiggle-print scarves, and Zandra herself, looking so cool with another extra-long scarf flung around her neck. This issue had another great photo of Zandra's friends Myroslava and Oxana Prystay dressed in print tunics over sheer pants. Myroslava also wore a flowing, tiered, printed handkerchief poncho. And a memorable photograph by Barry Berenson in *Vogue* in 1971, depicting Zandra with her shagged emerald-green hair tipped with feathers of fuchsia, purple and pink, her face painted in red and blue and dotted with gold and silver; she wears various outfits in front of her wallpaper line for Vice Versa.

The list goes on. In December of 1972, Bianca Jagger was photographed for the *Sunday Times Magazine*. On the cover she is wearing Zandra's pink 'Chevron Shawl' print butterfly dress. Inside, there is another version of that yellow, wool felt circular coat with multicoloured topstitching, and a dress in the black-and-white 'Sparkle' print, inspired by the Tudor-period zigzag slashing of fabric. The dress has a black satin front yoke with an asymmetrical opening. Bianca is shown lounging in a sea of pillows, and then painting her lips in the mirror, wearing a jade-green 'Field of Lilies' dress. This famous print was inspired by lilies given to Zandra by a friend when she was visiting Japan in 1971.

In 1973, Donna Mitchell was on the cover of the March issue of British *Vogue*, wearing a black felt circle coat with white trim and topstitching on the collar that swirls around her shoulders. On her head is perched a white pillbox hat elaborately beaded by Tina Chow with pearls, gold stars and black sequins. Ali McGraw, at her most beautiful, was wearing a red lettuce-edged jersey with yellow topstitching and blue beads on the cover of *Harper's Bazaar* in October 1972. And Art Kane did my favourite ever photo shoot of Zandra's clothes for *Viva* in February 1974. These carefully cut clippings were all the images that I had of Zandra's extraordinary fashions, style and world.

The invitation for the 'Circle in the Square' show had a cover with 'Zandra' handwritten millions of times by Zandra herself. The front cover had two pink bows. Inside the invitation 'thank you' was written many times over. The amazing Leonard did end up doing the hair, not only for all the models in the show, but also for Zandra. Barbara Daly did the make-up and masks, and Goody Two Shoes

opposite
Bianca Jagger wearing a Zandra Rhodes silk chiffon dress printed with 'Field of Lilies' design in a photo shoot for the *Sunday Times*, December 1972.
Photo: Eva Sereny.

above, top to bottom
Donna Mitchell wearing a Zandra Rhodes wool felt coat on the cover of British *Vogue*, March 1973. Hat: Tina Chow.
Photo: Clive Arrowsmith / Vogue © The Condé Nast Publications Ltd.
Ali McGraw wearing a Zandra Rhodes jersey top on the cover of *Harper's Bazaar*, October 1972.
Photo: Bill King / Harper's Bazaar © Hearst.

ZANDRA RHODES AS AN INSPIRATIONAL ICON

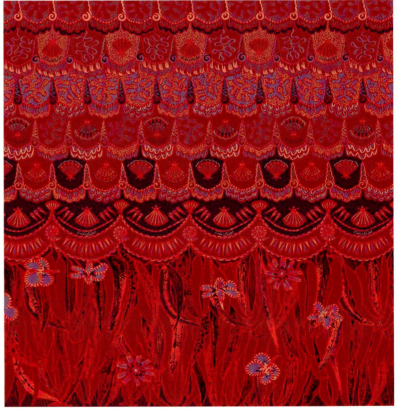

above, top to bottom
Model wearing a Zandra Rhodes printed wool felt cloak in a photo shoot for *Viva*, February 1974. Photo: Art Kane ©. Gigi Hadid walking in Anna Sui's Spring 2016 New York fashion show, wearing a dress printed with Zandra Rhodes's 'Tahiti' design. Photo: Victor Virgile.

above, top to bottom
Model wearing a Zandra Rhodes silk chiffon dress printed with 'Chevron Shawl' design in a photo shoot for *Viva*, February 1974. Photo: Art Kane ©. Zandra Rhodes, 'Tahiti' print design, 2015, for Anna Sui's Spring/Summer 2016 Tahitian collection.

(a New York-based company that made amazing platform shoes – everyone wore them to see The New York Dolls) provided the shoes.

Once again, Clive Arrowsmith shot the poster, this time an image of Marisa Berenson, in faded sepia tones with touches of pale pink and pistachio green, printed on beige card. And there was a fan that you could really use, drawn by Zandra and cut out and folded, with a pistachio satin ribbon printed with 'Zandra Rhodes' in pink. The same 'Button Flower' pattern from my own coat was the motif for the ceramic dishes used at the after-show dinner. These were made by Carol McNicoll and Zandra still has them today in her London penthouse.

As I mentioned, this was the first big fashion outing for me and Steve. When we descended the escalator, we arrived in a sea of Seventh Avenue designers and all of fashion society. The first person we saw was Donyale Luna, posing in a veiled harem outfit. The show was packed with well-known attendees: Diana Vreeland, DD Ryan, Elsa Peretti, Fernando Sánchez, Joe Eula, Diane von Furstenberg, Henri Bendel's Geraldine Stutz, Nan Kempner, Jane Forth, Joel Schumacher, Mica Ertegun, Chessy Rayner, Bill Blass, Pauline Trigère, Halston, Scott Barrie, Mary McFadden, Chester Weinberg, Ava Cherry (David Bowie's girlfriend), Martha of Martha's and Laura Johnson – to name just a few. Zandra's signature printed chiffons, the lettuce-edged silk jerseys, 'Field of Lilies' print dresses, Cinderella-like tulle gowns, the squiggles, the snail flowers, irides-cent seashell sequins, all floating by on legendary models: Donna Jordan with hot-pink hair, Pat Cleveland, Beatrice Welles, Apollonia, Chris Royer and Nancy North – the 'Halstonettes'.

These memories were crystallised in press pictures from the night. An image of Ruth and Paul was printed in a *New York Times* column from 24 April 1974, 'Fashion Talk', by Bernadine Morris. And a photo of Steven and me, shot by Bill Cunningham, later appeared in *Interview* magazine on the 'Pix Pix Pix' page in October 1992. Years later, Bill sent me a print of the photo; to this day, it is one of my most cherished gifts.

I now collect vintage clothes by Zandra at auction houses and vintage shops. I have often visited the Fashion and Textile Museum that Zandra founded (and lives above). During one of those visits, I was thrilled to finally meet Zandra and, over the years, we've developed a good friendship. I have even been able to order directly from her some of the dresses and prints that I missed out on the first time around: the 'Snail Flower' and 'Squiggle' patterns, and my all-time favourite, the 'Indian Feathers' print that Zandra created after a trip to New York, where she toured the National Museum of the American Indian. I love going to Zandra's studio, where they screen-print all the fabrics by hand, and, of course, her fabulous rainbow penthouse, where you are enchanted from the moment you step into her world.

Our friendship is also collaborative: in 2016 Zandra designed a print for my Spring/Summer Tahitian collection. She had just returned from a holiday in Tahiti and sent me the sketches she did during her travels. Using the exact same work process documented in her 1984 book, *The Art of Zandra Rhodes*, she designed me a print from the various elements – it is beautiful and classic Zandra. It's now my new favourite.

And finally, during another visit to the Fashion and Textile Museum, I met the director Celia Joicey, and we had coffee in the adjoining restaurant. At the end of my conversation with her, she asked if I would like to do an exhibition. So it was really Zandra who was instrumental in bringing about *The World of Anna Sui*, which made its debut at the museum in 2017. To top things off, Zandra and Twiggy were at the opening party, which made it a dream come true!

above, top to bottom
Marisa Berenson on the 1974 Zandra Rhodes poster.
Make-up: Barbara Daly. Hair: Leonard of London.
Porcelain hair ornaments: Carol McNicoll.
Photo: Clive Arrowsmith.
Anna Sui and Steven Meisel attending the Zandra Rhodes
'Circle in the Square' fashion show in New York, April 1974.
Photo: Bill Cunningham, courtesy of Anna Sui.

The decade of the 1980s saw Rhodes's collections increase in scope and technique. Printed and shaped silk chiffons remained a hallmark of her work, whilst fully beaded dresses, ball gowns and knitwear were introduced. A series of internationally inspired collections reflects the increasing travel and experiences of the designer.

Diana Ross wearing a Zandra Rhodes top from the 1981
'Renaissance/Gold' collection, New York, 9 September 1981.
Photo: Richard Avedon © The Richard Avedon Foundation.

1980–1989

this page and opposite (detail)
Spring/Summer 1980, 'Chinese' collection. Silk organza top printed with 'Chinese Squares' design, with a silk organza skirt printed with 'Scribble Border' design, with a stitched satin boned obi belt and beading on the pagoda sleeves, styles 79/124 (top) and 79/141 (skirt).

this page and opposite (detail)
Autumn/Winter 1980, 'Chinese Constructive' collection. Calf-length wool felt coat lined with satin, printed with 'Chinese Water Circles' design, embellished with lengths of plaited orange braid with Chinese-style metal tips, style 80/64.

pp. 68–69 (details)
left Spring/Summer 1981, 'African' collection. Blue pleated satin evening jacket printed with 'The Jungle Flower Stole' design, style 81/111.
right Spring/Summer 1981, 'African' collection. Pink pleated satin evening jacket printed with 'Mexican Border' design, style 81/76.

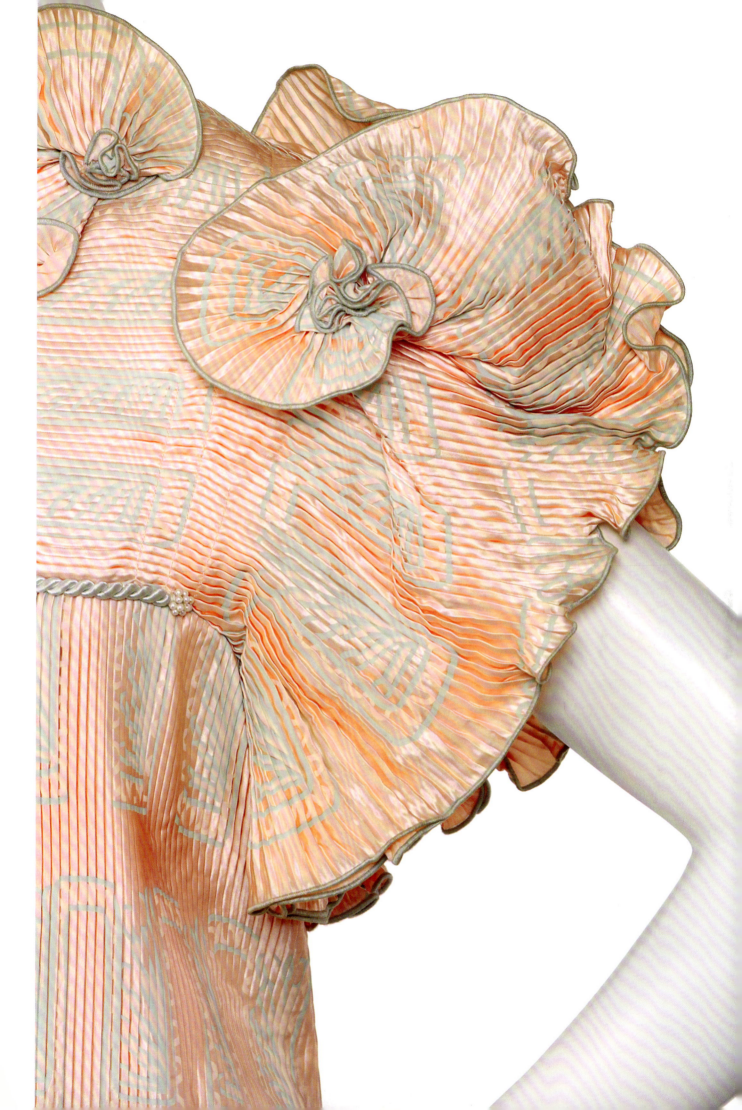

this page
Autumn/Winter 1981,
'Renaissance/Gold' collection.
Quilted satin corset printed
with 'Spinifix Landscape' design,
with gold lurex pleated swirl
sleeves, worn with separately
attached matching pleated
panniers over a full-length
pleated gold lurex skirt, worn
over a boned underskirt, styles
81/131 (corset), 81/47 (skirt)
and 81/150 (panniers).
    opposite
Autumn/Winter 1981,
'Renaissance/Gold' collection.
Pleated gold lurex jacket with
swirl sleeves and a tassel
embellished with gold beads,
style 81/178.

this page
Andrea Dellal wearing a short ruched evening dress
from the Spring/Summer 1982 'Fairy' collection.
Photo: Stan Ripton.

opposite
Spring/Summer 1982, 'Fairy' collection. Silk taffeta evening
dress with fitted corset-styled bodice and ruched skirt,
printed with 'Frilly Circle' design, style 82/33.

Autumn/Winter 1982, 'The Indian' collection. Wool cloak with wide gold-embroidered braid neckband and ultrasuede trim, printed with 'Indian Border Stripe' design, style 82/111.

above
Pat Cleveland wearing a short wool sari-style
wrap dress, worn with black *choli* crop top
and black narrow trousers from 'The Indian'
collection, backstage at the Autumn/Winter
1982 fashion show. Hat: Stephen Jones.
Make-up: Yvonne Gold.
Photo: Robyn Beeche.
below
Pat Cleveland wearing a white cloak from
'The Indian' collection, backstage at the
Autumn/Winter 1982 fashion show. Snood:
Stephen Jones. Make-up: Yvonne Gold.
Photo: Robyn Beeche.

1980–1989

opposite
Models in ruched jersey dresses with bows,
worn with ruched jersey trousers with seams
on the outside, from 'The Indian' collection,
backstage at the Autumn/Winter 1982
fashion show. Brooch on headpiece: Andrew
Logan. Make-up: Yvonne Gold.
Photo: Robyn Beeche.

this page
Autumn/Winter 1982, 'The Indian' collection.
Sleeveless dress with large collar in ruffled
silk taffeta that extends in the back to a
deep neckline, finished with a large bow,
style 82/140.

ZANDRA RHODES: 50 FABULOUS YEARS IN FASHION

Spring/Summer 1983, 'Mount
Olympus' collection. Silk chiffon
gown printed with 'Indian Border
Stripe' design, with sari-style
shoulder drape and decorative
knot at the shoulder, style 83/58.

this page and opposite (detail)
Spring/Summer 1983, 'Mount Olympus' collection. Silk chiffon gown
with hand beading, bodice printed with 'Reverse Paisley' design and
skirt with the 'Pyramids' design, worn with a satin sash, style 83/72.

this page
Spring/Summer 1983, 'Mount Olympus' collection. Close-up
of suede bodice with pinked edges, punched and printed with
'Indian Circle' design, style 83/59.
opposite
Models wearing raw silk dresses with suede bodices from the
'Mount Olympus' collection, backstage at the Spring/Summer
1983 fashion show. Hats: Stephen Jones.
Photo: Robyn Beeche.

opposite
Autumn/Winter 1983, 'Medieval' collection. Apron in dip-dyed silk chiffon printed with 'Indian Square' design, gold edged with pearls, with leather straps and gold punched and ornamented leather panel. Parma-violet rayon jersey slip with flowing silk chiffon sleeves printed with 'Frilly Circle' design and edged with pearls, styles 83/223 (apron), 83/170 (slip) and 83/208 (jacket).

this page (top)
Carmen Squire posing for the 1983 Zandra Rhodes poster. Make-up: Phyllis Cohen. Hair with mesh snood: Robert Lobetta. Photo: Robyn Beeche.

this page (bottom)
Model walking in Zandra Rhodes retrospective catwalk show at Paris Fashion Week, Fall 2012. Make-up: MAC. Photo: Patrick Anderson.

opposite
Purple jersey dress with leather bustier from the 'Medieval' collection,
backstage at the Autumn/Winter 1983 fashion show. Hair with mesh
snood: Leonard of London. Photo: Robyn Beeche.

this page
Autumn/Winter 1983, 'Medieval' collection. Purple jersey dress
with punched leather bustier with seams on the outside, attached
to a full-length skirt narrowing towards the hemline, style 82/224.

1980–1989

87

this page

Autumn/Winter 1983, 'Medieval' collection. Close-up: Off-the-shoulder silk chiffon full-length evening dress, with three gold leather straps holding up the bodice and the centre strap leading to a gold punched leather decorative pointed collar (front and back) cut to the shape of the 'Indian Square' design, ornamented with purple rhinestones and embellished with strips of diamanté, beads and sequins, style 83/172.

opposite

Michele Paradise wearing a silk chiffon gown from the 'Medieval' collection, backstage at the Autumn/Winter 1983 fashion show. Hair with mesh snood: Leonard of London. Photo: Robyn Beeche.

Zandra Rhodes in a long black tunic from the 'Magic Carpet'
collection, backstage at the Autumn/Winter 1984 fashion show.
Photo: Robyn Beeche.

Autumn/Winter 1984, 'Magic Carpet' collection. Long tunic with elbow-length sleeves in black silk georgette and a low back neckline, hand-beaded using zari-work technique with silver sequins and bugle beads in the 'Playing Cards' design; hand-beaded matching trousers; styles 84/177 (tunic) and 87/173 (trousers).

this page
Model in a silk chiffon evening dress printed with 'Manhattan'
design and embellished with diamanté and satin belt from the
Spring/Summer 1985 'Images of Woman' collection, style 85/55.
Photo: Robyn Beeche.

opposite
'Manhattan' screen-print in three colours.

opposite
Beaded 'Manhattan' dress from the 'India Revisited' collection, backstage at the Autumn/Winter 1985 fashion show. Hair: Trevor Sorbie. Make-up: Phyllis Cohen. Photo: Robyn Beeche.

this page
Autumn/Winter 1985, 'India Revisited' collection. Hand-beaded 'Manhattan' knee-length evening dress, with elbow-length sleeves and a high rounded neckline with low back drape, style 85/196. Kindly donated by Martha Gafford.

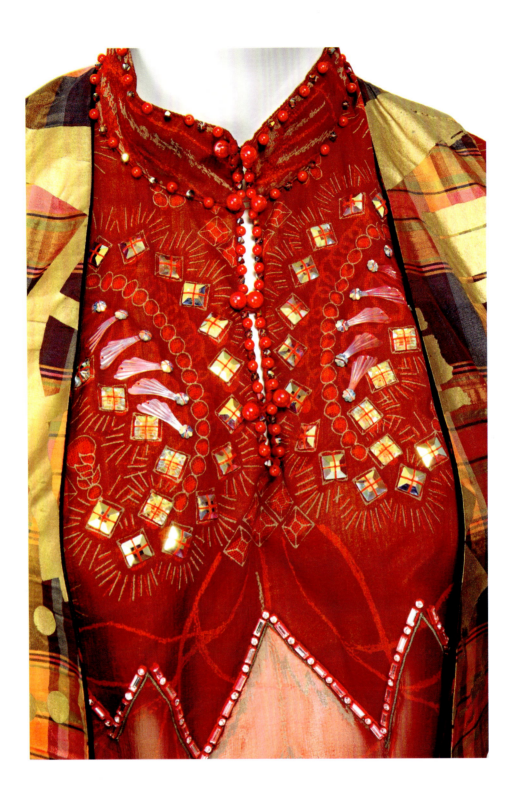

this page

Autumn/Winter 1985, 'India Revisited' collection. Close-up: Three-piece evening ensemble consisting of lined silk chiffon trousers; a matching tunic with dolman sleeves and a mandarin collar, heavily embellished across the lined zig zag yoke and printed with 'Peacock Frills' design; worn with a silk taffeta waistcoat printed with gold 'Cubist Brush Stroke' design; styles 85/153 (tunic), 85/177 (waistcoat) and 85/170 (trousers).

opposite

Joanna Thomas wearing a three-piece evening ensemble from the 'India Revisited' collection, backstage at Autumn/Winter 1985 fashion show (mirrored front and back views). Hair: Trevor Sorbie. Make-up: Phyllis Cohen. Photos: Robyn Beeche.

Models in silk chiffon gowns printed with 'Reverse Peacock' design,
with stitched satin waistbands, from the 1985 'India Revisited' collection,
walking in the 1985 show. Hair: Trevor Sorbie. Make-up: Phyllis Cohen.
Model on right: Michele Paradise. Photo: Robyn Beeche.

opposite

'Peacock Godet' design printed in three colours on silk chiffon.
Photo: Student project at UCA managed by Piers Atkinson.

ZANDRA RHODES: 50 FABULOUS YEARS IN FASHION

pp. 104–105
left Spring/Summer 1987, 'Secrets of the Nile' collection.
Close-up: Hand-beaded silk georgette dress with hand-rolled hem
embroidered with 'Pyramids' and 'Egyptian Stars' designs, style 87/125.
right Hand-beaded silk georgette dress from the 'Secrets of the
Nile' collection, backstage at the Spring/Summer 1987 fashion show
(mirrored, front and back). Make-up: Phyllis Cohen. Hair: Trevor Sorbie.
Photo: Robyn Beeche.

this page
Silk chiffon top and trousers from the 'Secrets of the Nile' collection,
backstage at the Spring/Summer 1987 fashion show. Make-up:
Phyllis Cohen. Hair: Trevor Sorbie.
Photo: Robyn Beeche.
opposite
'Tutankhamun's Leopard' design printed on silk chiffon.
Photo: Student project at UCA managed by Piers Atkinson.

this page
Autumn/Winter 1987, 'Wish Upon a Star' collection.
Close-up: Evening dress with net to both line and support the sleeves; skirt stiffened with several layers of net and printed with 'All Over Stars' design, style 87/220.

opposite
Persephoné wearing a net dress from the 'Wish Upon a Star' collection, private photo shoot in 1987.
Photo: Christopher Bissell.

this page and opposite (detail)
Autumn/Winter 1987, 'Wish Upon
a Star' collection. Silk chiffon
evening dress printed with 'All
Over Stars' design, with hand-
beaded, twisted rouleau neckline;
long fitted sleeves with beaded
trim; lined bodice and knee-length
skirt in tiers of ruffles with beading
to the peplum; style 87/86.
The 'All Over Stars' print design
has been used throughout with
the border, emphasising the
shoulder line, peplum and skirt
hem. The skirt and peplum are
both supported by a layer of net.
A version of this dress was worn
by Elizabeth Taylor (see p. 52).

ZANDRA RHODES: 50 FABULOUS YEARS IN FASHION

Bianca Jagger
François de Menil &
Zandra

Zandra fitting Diana
Ross

Zandra with Natalie
Wood

Gianni Versace
with J·A·Q in Zandra.

Zandra
Diana Vreeland
& Andy Warhol

Emmanuelle Khanh
J·A·Q and Zandra

Zandra
with Joan & Jack
& David Hockney

Helmut Berger
Valentino
& J·A·Q

Zandra Rhodes
and
Karl Lagerfeld

Photographs in this essay are courtesy of Joan Agajanian Quinn.

THE ADVENTURES OF ZANDRA RHODES AND JOAN QUINN: ART, HOLLYWOOD AND POP CULTURE

Joan Agajanian Quinn

In the late 1970s, all the English hotshots wanted to come to Los Angeles. We held everyone's interest because of the weather, the art colonies and, of course, Hollywood. A lot of people came back and forth, one of whom was designer Zandra Rhodes. My husband and I were considered hotshots too; Jack was the president of the Los Angeles County Bar Association, the youngest ever, and we were feeling very sophisticated.

Our friend the artist Billy Al Bengston had exchanged houses with London-based painter Allen Jones, who lived in Fulham, and we planned to visit him after a trip to Paris. On our visit, Billy took Jack and me to meet Zandra at her Porchester Road studio. Zandra was gracious and showed us around; I asked about the clothes and when I found out the prices, my Beverly Hills reaction was: 'I could buy a James Galanos on sale at Amelia Gray on Rodeo Drive for that amount of money and he is far more known than Zandra!' So I said I'd think about it, and we left. When we got back to the hotel, low and behold, I had forgotten my Instamatic, or was it my Minolta? Then, when I went back, Zandra and I had a wonderful chat and I invited her to visit me on her next trip to California. Little did I know what Zandra had in the works then. A couple of months later, she arrived in Los Angeles. As I write, that was exactly 50 years ago. How do I remember? Restaurateur Michael Chow recently celebrated his 50 years in Beverly Hills and Zandra used to show at Charles Gallay's store on Camden Drive, across the street from Chow's restaurant. She had one spectacular and memorable show where the models dressed in the shop, crossed the street and walked an elevated plank into Mr. Chow's. From this event on, Mr Chow's became the hot new addition to the Beverly Hills landscape, once again tying the swinging Londoners to privileged Angelenos.

Jack and I didn't know it at the time, but we were called a 'power couple'. Jack was thriving in the Bar Association and I was involved in many art projects, the most important being my appointment to the prestigious California Arts Council by flamboyant, fashion-conscious San Francisco assemblyman Willie Brown, and my position as the West Coast editor for Andy Warhol's *Interview* magazine. Back home in Los Angeles, my husband, two identical twin daughters, Jennifer and Amanda, and I lived in a 1930s, Mediterranean-style Beverly Hills house that, prior to our moving in, had been lived in by actor Oliver Hardy, famed television host Ed Sullivan and Oscar-nominated songwriter Mack David. We loved our house, but called on decorator Philip Miller to help save the good features while giving it a refresh. After some quick fixes on

the house I launched a series of salons in our living room, which included artists like Ed Moses, Bob Graham and Bengston, and the artists and celebrities' girlfriends Anjelica Huston, Teri Garr, Samantha Eggar, Candy Clark and Mary Kay Place. When Divine was in Los Angeles we would put on posh tea parties. Divine would always pick out the cakes – his favourites were coconut cake and banana cream pie. Philip would set the dining-room table with Chinese porcelains filled with cookies and flowers. Friends who joined us included Emmanuelle Khanh, Michèle Lamy, Ed Ruscha, Quentin Crisp, David Hockney, Jean-Michel Basquiat, Laura Elizabeth 'Little Nell' Campbell, Tab Hunter, Bob Colacello, Christopher Isherwood and Don Bachardy. Zandra met, mixed and mingled with our social, legal and art-world friends. So it went: judges loved to study her, lawyers were awed by her, artists felt a kinship with her and, of course, the social hostesses of the day wanted to flaunt Zandra's designs and invite her to their extravagant parties.

On several occasions, our friend the architect Frank Gehry had guests to his bachelor pad. Zandra, of course, loved going there and she remembers one night when Frank brought the dinner to the table: my husband Jack looked quizzically at Frank and, with his typical irreverent humour, asked 'Frank, are you still serving that lousy food?' Then the table of artists burst out in laughter. Zandra instantly charmed people on the Los Angeles scene: singers Steve Lawrence and Eydie Gormé, who wore Zandra's designs on stage, loved having Zandra over. We met many times for lunch or for tea with Eydie and her friends – sometimes just to confer on a special-order gown for a charity show or on what would be a knockout for Las Vegas or New York.

In 1976, I attended the wedding of the year wearing my beautiful Zandra Rhodes chiffon: actress and model Marisa Berenson was marrying industrialist James Randall. The chic affair was held at a private Beverly Hills mansion and my date was none other than Andy Warhol. The event was attended not only by Hollywood celebrities, but also by a host of designers like Gianni Versace and Valentino Garavani. I dazzled them all in my red Zandra Rhodes gown and every time someone would compliment me on my dress, Andy would ask when Zandra was going to advertise in *Interview*. Andy was always thinking about selling ads and making money. Many of the wedding guests already had Warhol portraits, but he was still looking for commissions from the others.

Zandra also came to many of the lunches that my husband and I hosted in the exclusive, darkly panelled Directors' Room at the Santa Anita racetrack. She didn't bet on the horses, but our guests were always buying tickets for her. During one such lunch, I introduced Zandra to Contessa Cohen – a southern belle with perfectly coiffed blazing red hair and a daily application of make-up by the experts from Aida Grey salon on Wilshire Boulevard. Contessa was in the running to be one of the grand dames of entertainment, and was looking to take the position of official Beverly Hills hostess to Zandra Rhodes. She, with her real-estate mogul husband Dan, loved hosting parties. Zandra was the guest of honour at formal black-tie soirées hosted by the Cohens at the Bistro on Canon Drive; these dinners, for about 200 guests, included members of the social elite like Nancy Reagan and Ann Miller. They were lavish affairs with an orchestra, specially designed hostess gifts and handmade place cards, held in a room filled with fresh flowers and with trees surrounding the dance floor. Everything was provided by Harry Finley, Contessa's special florist and party-planner. Zina Hoffman from the famous meat-packing family; Miriam Parks, whose husband was the plastic surgeon to the stars; and other friends from the Hillcrest Country Club were in attendance with the likes of Hollywood's Joan Collins and Zsa Zsa Gabor.

Contessa also had lunches for Zandra after her shopping sprees at department store Neiman Marcus. The store manager of the Beverly Hills branch, the brilliant and always gracious John Martens, was sometimes asked to invite some of his Neiman Marcus clientele. Contessa kept a close eye on who should be included as she was protecting her exclusive hold on the guest of honour. There was no competition in Los Angeles as to who had the largest closet full of Zandra's frocks – it was Contessa, hands down. Meanwhile, I had a wardrobe by Zandra but also friends like Issey Miyake, Emmanuelle Khanh and Michèle Lamy.

Once, Zandra and I were driving to my house after one of Contessa's bistro luncheons and I saw Diana Ross driving into her garage on Elevado Avenue. Zandra had met Diana the night before so I stopped the car and told Zandra to go say hello. Zandra jumped out of the car and walked up the sidewalk but Diana shouted, 'If you come one step closer I'll close the garage door on you!' We were stunned and Zandra got back into the car shaking. We drove a few blocks to my home on Alta Drive and told Jack the story. We all laughed and wondered how and why Diana had changed her tune with Zandra from one day to the next. The next morning while we were having coffee, the phone rang. It was Diana: 'Hello, this is Diana Ross. Sorry about yesterday . . . can I come over and look at some clothes?' She came over in sweats and no make-up and explained that when she first met Zandra, Zandra was wearing an exotic white turban and chic chiffon, so that when Zandra approached her with her green hair with feathers on the end flying in the breeze, Diana freaked out – she thought it was a hippie trying to stalk her. Diana had heard that Zandra was at the forefront of the new punk revolution and wanted to see something from that collection. Needless to say, she went home with her arms full!

Zandra always had something creative to share, be it a new headwrap, cut-outs of her fabrics to pin on as accessories, the latest brooch by Andrew Logan, a new colour for her hair, or an extraordinary new eyebrow shape. Our friend groups merged: Andrew Logan, Duggie Fields and Allen Jones with John Waters, Larry Hagman and Paul Ruscha. We kept a tight-knit group as we flew back and forth between Heathrow and Los Angeles. So many stories to share.

Zandra's decorator friend Maxine Smith, who used Zandra's fabrics when decorating her flat in London and who was married in a Zandra Rhodes gown, lived in the canyon with her husband Gary, the legendary television producer. Max and her then-business partner were known as interior decorators to the stars – people like Henry Winkler, Olivia Newton-John, and Barbra Streisand. Zandra and I were invited to Maxine's baby shower at the Hillcrest Country Club and Zandra took the limelight even from Streisand.

So, there we were in the midst of what was happening and, may I say, we were probably making it happen. I was privy to great inside gossip, interesting information about the art world and press secrets about celebrity clients; all of which meant I could contribute and disperse my information to the media world with conviction! I was writing for *Interview*, *Los Angeles* magazine and *L.A. Style* magazine, and appearing on television to talk about the art and fashion scene. I was so lucky to have such great material to write about.

In the late 1970s, Zandra surprised us by dating Eric Douglas. I became very close to his mother, Anne, and spent time with her and Kirk Douglas at their Rexford Drive home. Anne and I went to New York City to see Eric, who was starring in an off-Broadway play. He had found his place on the stage and was dating an accomplished young woman. When I look back on those days, we were the precursor of social reality shows, only the action was written about in newspapers. Former *Women's Daily* West Coast editor Jody Jacobs became the society editor of the *Los Angeles Times* and wrote an ongoing series of columns about all these social events. Marylou Luther, the fashion editor of the *Los Angeles Times*, always found an interesting fashion-related story about Zandra, whether it was a new hemline, an exotic fabric design or a different way of beading appliqué.

The 1980s exploded in many ways – food, fashion, arts, movie stars and directors. One of our favourite people was director Ron Link. Ron was a friend of Divine and had worked with him in New York City, London and Los Angeles on the play *Women Behind Bars*. Ron also directed Zandra's famous 1980 'Fantasy Fashion' show at La Jolla Contemporary Art Museum (now the Museum of Contemporary Art San Diego). This theatrical runway show brought another dimension to the catwalk, using objects like oranges and palm leaves; Ron caught the eye of the audience with his slow ballet choreography, like a sequence of dreams floating down the runway.

By the late 1980s, Zandra had made many trips to Los Angeles and I'd made many trips to London. I had become a Zandra Rhodes ambassador: a client, a curator, a press agent, a loyal confidant and a dear friend. I found myself the faithful advocate of an extraordinary talent. Together we travelled all around the United

Zandra and Barbara
Nessim

Contessa Cohen
Zandra and J.A.Q.

Zandra with
Bob Graham

Zandra with Ron Link

Zandra with
DEREK BOSHIER

Ed Ruscha
J.A.Q (wearing Zandra)
and Michael Chow

Issey Miyake
J.A.Q + Zandra

Zandra
Paloma Picasso
and J.A.Q

J.A.Q (wearing Zandra)
with Frank Gehry

Maxine Smith (wearing Zandra) Zandra & Barbra Streisand

Zandra with Edith Head

Eydie Gormé and Zandra

Divine, Zandra Billy Al Bengston & Ned Evans

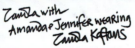

Zandra with Amanda & Jennifer wearing Zandra Kaftans

J.A.Q, Zandra Dennis Hopper & Paige Rense

Duggie Fields and Zandra

Zandra Larry & Heidi Hagman & J.A.Q

Kirk Douglas and Zandra

States – to New York City, Houston and Dallas in Texas, Scottsdale in Arizona, and more.

During our travels to Manhattan we shared time with Joe Lombardo, a talented graphic designer who lived in a large Upper West Side apartment. The apartment was such a personal statement of luxurious originality that *House and Garden* published the story I submitted on it with a big spread! My Condé Nast mentor, Lloyd Ziff, was the art and design director for *House and Garden* at the time and was excited to add the off-beat glamour of Joe Lombardo to their pages. Joe never failed to entertain Zandra and her friends with lively dinner parties; friends like artist Barbara Nessim, who was one of the first computer artists and an influence on Zandra's head drawings, and Frankie Piazza, who was working as a dresser to Divine. Frankie eventually moved to Hollywood to assist Whoopi Goldberg and work on films, most notably 1982's hit *Tootsie* with Dustin Hoffman.

One night around 11.30 pm, after a riotous, chatter-filled dinner, there was a knock at Joe's door. A man in a black chauffeur's uniform announced that the car was ready. When Joe came back into the dining room, Zandra had donned a black wig and was out the door for a midnight rendezvous. She swept past us wearing a black cape to match her wig and went out into the night, leaving us to ponder the transformation. So many questions! Some time later, we finally solved the mystery. Unbeknown to us, this mystery date was Salah Hassanein, then president of Warner Bros. International Theatres (and now Zandra's partner of more than 30 years). She would disguise herself because she didn't want to be recognised on their nights out on the town.

Even today Zandra and I remain great friends, with a wealth of memories between us: the creative spirit never quits, it's alive and well as we fly back and forth between Heathrow and LAX, remembering the oh-so-many stories we've lived, and eagerly awaiting more to come.

'ON MY LADY UNLIKE ANY': ZANDRA RHODES'S INFLUENCE ON THE INDIAN FASHION INDUSTRY

Rajeev Sethi

A to Z, Zandra is quite complete. Constant beginnings leave stories with no end. Forever evolving, Zandra is simply amazing! Here is an alphabetic deconstruction of Zandra Rhodes and India, through a lens from the East.

A for *Aditi*, appliqué and Andrew Logan

The 1980s began with a bold, transdisciplinary expression of the state of Indian arts and crafts. The seminal Festival of India brought 19 exhibitions, and accompanying performances, lectures and seminars, to the UK in 1982, showcasing India's ancient treasures and confident, contemporary creative culture. Co-organised by the two nations' governments, it reinvigorated creative establishments in the subcontinent as well as acting as an expression of 'soft power' abroad (though I prefer the phrase 'compelling diplomacy'). Preparing for my own contribution to this grand project – a wide-reaching exhibition of Indian crafts and culture – and with the support of my formidable mentor, Mrs Pupul Jayakar, I went looking for Zandra's talent in order to connect with new, market-friendly design sensibilities and to help transform the reach of traditional skills. The Festivals of India (they were held not only in the UK, but in countries including France, the United States and Russia) would assess how time-honoured vocabularies could form an entirely new language, inciting worldwide attention. Disruptive ideas were flying on our very first meeting. Enthusiastically agreeing to collaborate on the last section of my exhibition, titled *Aditi*, Zandra even dressed up for a poster, writing 'Aditi' on her forehead. Our subsequent travels all over India and the resulting collaborations opened to rave reviews. We got an entirely new perspective, creating the opportunity to pursue innovative enterprises.

Aditi, which had a troubled gestation at the Barbican in central London, was based on the theme of rites of passage. Transmitting India's creative and cultural skills, with a particular emphasis on 'little' traditions, sparked an expansive discourse. Generation after generation of the skilled poor living in scattered villages in India has strived against great odds to sustain a profound legacy, fast turning fragile. At this time, the potential for reinvention needed to be positioned in the global context. The power of vital skills rarely witnessed outside of rural India lay latent. Another India – not confined to starving kids with bloated bellies and grand Maharajas on caparisoned elephants – was waiting for an emotional and creative encounter with the West. Zandra recognises *humsafars* (fellow travellers) and for her very first trip to India in 1981, she could find no one as appropriate as artist Andrew Logan to accompany her.

Photo of Andrew Logan taken by Zandra Rhodes while shopping in India, 1981.

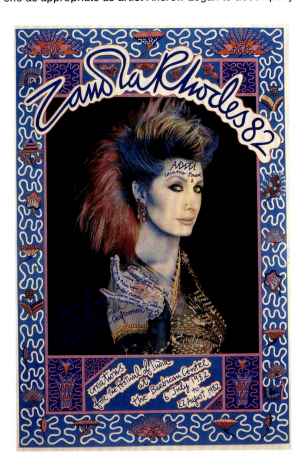

Zandra Rhodes 1982 poster. Make-up: Yvonne Gold. Earrings: Andrew Logan. Photo: Robyn Beeche.

B for block printing, butterflies and books

For *Aditi*, handmade, block-printed banners with exploding trees of life appeared under the Barbican's new atriums. Zandra's huge designs, the blocks for which were carved in specially treated wood in the Indian city of Farrukhabad, were used in a free play of scale, combined with her signature squiggles. There were Z-shaped tables upholstered with fabrics in zari- and zardozi-work, wild cushions on bedcovers with appliqué and embroideries, and into these snuggled mannequins in sequinned silks. By 1984, Zandra's first book laying out her hugely innovative clothing was published – formed and structured as never before, the garments were luminescent, silhouetted against a white background. The precious collection of dresses, laid out like butterflies, flew out each time a page turned!

C for carpet and cross-cultural constructs

The German government commissioned me to design the scenography for a themed pavilion on the concept of 'Basic Needs' for Expo 2000 in Hanover. In an effort to make the fair universal, one was encouraged to collaborate with international talent in informing German industry. I chose Zandra, two Australian Aboriginal artists, Mary McFadden from the United States, Parvaneh Itemadi from Iran and Andrey Bartenev from Russia to work with the German manufacturer Vorwerk. We devised a way to produce designs for machine-made carpets that, although printed in factories, could pay for craftspeople living in cottages to create bespoke products for the market. Sustaining skilled livelihoods is a 'basic need' and Zandra could be put into the creative crucible once again to explore and experiment in this field. Zandra's own design was based on the waq waq motif – the 'speaking tree' design seen on Mughal carpets. Reflecting the most inspiring Jain philosophy of *jiv daya*, which describes acts of compassion for all living things, we opened a Pandora's box of new iconographies. Turtles became rabbits as birds turned predators and deer pounced as tigers with the magic

ease that only Zandra's paintbrush and cross-cultural creative imagination could invent.

Yet another historic tree of life was unleashed as repeats of carpet yardage, resonant with an intuitive appreciation of the cosmic interdependence of flora and fauna. We also made bespoke carved screens and *peedies* (low chairs) to complement the whole scenario.

D for Design with a capital 'D'

Tradition finds no word for design in the hundreds of languages and thousands of dialects of India. Design, as an all-encompassing but elusive concept, may be found like a wayward dog that doesn't belong until it is willing to stay at home. The word *sangeet* suggests music together with dance and drama. What it invokes is the uniquely Indian concept of *rasa*, suggesting the essence of an aesthetic experience, infused with the primeval sap of emotion. When manifested in shared experiences it goes beyond academic description. Zandra was able to express this idea beautifully in her India-inspired collections of 1982 and 1985 and her sari collection of 1987.

E for embroidery and embellishments

Motifs develop varied narratives and a variety of stitches create vocabularies that can embellish any bespoke apparel. Zandra, with her fabulous beaded dresses and saris, has been able to employ lots of women and men in South India, putting their skills to good use in manifesting dreams for people all over the world.

F for food and feasts

While cooking food, Zandra really relaxes. Like a squirrel, she remembers what is stored where and for how long in a tiny, open kitchen. Her green pea soup with roasted burnt sesame seeds is like nectar after a hard day of work. Her parties, put together generously and spontaneously, happen like magic. She comes from work an hour before her guests; Andrew Logan's bejewelled candelabras light up Carol McNicoll's ceramic crockery, making hers a fantasy table setting and the stage for unbridled camaraderie.

This alchemy of homemade food, dramatic ambience, a deep sense of hospitality and Zandra's dashing persona produce the charming recipe for an original cordon bleu experience. Whether

Zandra Rhodes, hand-painted and hand-carved screen.
Photo: Dakota Amber Scoppettuolo.

Hand-painted and hand-carved chairs (*peedies*) in Zandra Rhodes's rainbow penthouse. Photo: Patrick Anderson.

enjoying a culinary feast at high table or the frugal pleasure of street food, Zandra's tastebuds are alive, healthy and all-inclusive, demonstrating an innate creativity that expands far beyond the drawing board.

G for green cucumbers

In December 1987 it's 44 degrees centigrade in the shade; we're in a Jonga jeep with open windows passing through the dusty villages of the state of Odisha. Zandra spots a street vendor peeling fresh cucumbers on the roadside. Red chillies mixed with rock salt with a dash of lemon quench our thirst like little else. After a morning spent with Kishangarh's last painter making *pich-wais* (devotional pictures depicting the deity Krishna), we plough through Rajasthan's hot desert on our way to Makrana looking for pure white marble for a tabletop. Dry *akra* bushes and *kikar* trees stand lopped of all green branches, like gnarled fingers rising to a relentless noon sky. We stop to see a family digging a well in a moonscape. As we get out of the car, we see them start their one meal of the day: a dry roti, a horseradish and some salt. Seeing us approach, they break the white tuber in half and insist we share a bite each.

H for Hyderabad and homespun truths

Hyderabad was the city where Zandra was flown to judge Miss India in 1982 for an audience of 130 million! And here are some homespun truths: karma yoga is better than ritual worship. Small beginnings with big ideas are better than big dreams with no means. Attitude and snobs are boring. Keep it wild and simple but doable. Sketchbooks are easier than files.

I for India, inspiration and ikats

Zandra has responded to the creative stimulus that comes with travel like few design leaders before. She transforms what she

Rhodes's sketch of the dry *akra* brushes and *kikar* trees in India, 1987.

sees and experiences into profound expressions of artistic brilliance. She provokes hidebound 'traditionalists' but does not belittle time-honoured practices. The warp of intuition with the weft of skill, if programmed with imagination, can create complex forms and patterns like an incredible double ikat. During my voyages around India with Zandra, I introduced her to the ikat weavers in Odisha. Zandra toyed with the idea of transferring her well-known print motifs to ikats.

J for Jaipur, *jamdani* fabric and jali trellis

Jaipur is where Zandra shopped and shopped, discovering multi-hued beads for her bejewelled sari designs. And the possibilities of a *jamdani*, with its extra, non-structural weft thread, are myriad: the technique forms a kind of loom embroidery that negotiates light and shade with varying densities of pattern. It creates air-like fabric that resembles dappled sunshine – even moonshine – filtering through trellis. Intricate patterns appear on the floating mul cottons that Zandra loves to print. When held up to the sun they appear as intricate jali trellises, and, when on the floor, like elaborate inlays. Patterns etch themselves in the mind; not inside, not outside – liminal celebrations evoking the senses.

K for Kashmir

Time ceases as Zandra, Andrew and myself float down the Dal lake for hours in a shikara – a houseboat. Kashmir has sown potent seeds deep within each of us. Sprout they will, when the time and occasion present themselves. No seed is shy of germination. As the Sufi poet Amir Khusro had it of Kashmir: *Gar Firdaus bar-rue*

Rhodes's sketch of a boat on a lake in India, 1982.

zamin ast, hami asto, hamin asto, hamin ast ('If there be paradise on Earth – it is this and this and truly this').

L for London

London is a place of first stirrings; a steep learning curve with goals set, targets devised and plenty of opportunities to jump high; and it is Zandra's home, where she has embedded her roots in fashion and design. Within the heart of London is Zandra's triune: her company, where she creates bold prints and intricate designs; her rainbow penthouse, fabulously decorated with all colours of the spectrum; and the Fashion and Textile Museum, which she founded, exhibiting work from the world's leading designers.

M for mosaic floors

Cement floors reinforced with marble chips were *de rigueur* in most Indian homes until the last decade – the Italians developed an art form out of making architectural features with mosaic: fireplaces, furniture and Art Deco ornaments. Zandra once introduced me to her Australian friend, David Humphries – mosaic and terrazzo star from Sydney, Australia – who later fashioned the entrance floors for London's Fashion and Textile Museum, designed by the Mexican architect Ricardo Legorreta. These cement floors, decorated with marble 'jewels' and playful shapes, express the contemporaneity of old materials made new. This has taught me the importance of spontaneous wit and humour to complement high-end interiors.

Rhodes's mosaic floor entrance hall designed by David Humphries.
Photo: Kelly Robinson.

N for naps

One was warned before meeting Zandra that she could go off to sleep mid-sentence. Sleep she can – at any moment, though not when not required. She can be alert 24 hours a day, almost 7 days at a stretch if contingencies dictate. The evening after we met, we were at a friend's party, where the living room had giant pouffes upholstered by Zandra. We both sat bantering unnoticed and were found fast asleep when dinner was announced.

O for organisation, opera and Operation Luggage Island

Her multitasking transcontinental flair requires an organised mind and multidisciplinary aptitude; Zandra can always accommodate and allocates no time to complain. A constantly open mind means being on a perpetual learning curve, with an uncanny ability to recognise the sap as it rises (*rasa*, again). Whether costumes and sets for *Aida*, *The Magic Flute* and *The Pearl Fishers* (see pp. 149–55); inventing designs for bejewelled dragons on flying tapestries for the luggage island in Mumbai's International Airport; or dancing with folk artists, she plods on and yet sails through like a breeze.

P for pink hair

With her pink hair, Zandra has a magic key that has allowed her entry into amazing private places all over India. In remote villages, even old ladies want to touch her hair to know it's real. After all, as Diana Vreeland said, 'Pink is the navy blue of India!'

Q for quintessential optimist

Times can be tough. As one gets older, one finds running twice as hard is required just to stay in the same place. Nevertheless, Zandra's glass remains half full. She is always ready to take on the world. With a deep sense of commitment and responsibility – especially towards friends and colleagues – she continues to design and inspire with aplomb.

Andrew Logan, Robyn Beeche, Rajeev Sethi and Zandra Rhodes posing with maquette of Rhodes's design for 'Luggage Island' in Mumbai Airport, 2015.

R for Robyn Beeche and renewal

Those iconic annual posters that indisputably position Zandra's profound influence on the fashion-scape came from the hard work and creative eye of the formidably talented photographer Robyn Beeche. Together with Andrew Logan, Zandra and Robyn formed the band of musketeers last seen together in India as my dearest *humsafars*, in a journey that has yet to be completed. Robyn is now at peace in her divine space, leaving behind a collection of incredible photographic memories memorialising some of Zandra's most beautiful work.

Renewal is Zandra's mantra, like my mother's – both women doing more with less. My torn *kurtas* are reincarnated as dusters. I saw the carpet Zandra created for my Hanover exhibit (see 'C for carpet') reborn wall-to-wall in her apartment. Excess fabrics from her collections line rooms and staircases in her new home, in which I have had the privilege of staying and have seen refurbished. With a blink of her eyes and some glitter, Zandra renews her very being. From a hard working day she can dress up in a jiffy to start any evening.

S for saris

India's unstitched garment is the subliminal intellectual property of its weavers, working with their hands on all sorts of looms across the subcontinent. Skilfully divided into sections over varying lengths and widths, the sari's eternal structure and iconic wearing styles, with motifs woven, printed and embellished, unfolds an ancient magic. Enter Zandra in the 1980s. The allure of a rich context fast disappearing provokes saucy interventions: the sari spangled or combined with Victorian crinolines; *kanjivaram* (traditional silk saris) squiggled with sequinned embroideries running over brocade borders; *cholis* (short-sleeved bodices) with shoulder pads; beaded embroidered holes cut into *pallus* (the 'loose' ends of saris) allowing arms to go through and for the head to peek out without a veil!

S is also for shock, seduction, and for stupefying shows in Bombay (now Mumbai) and Delhi in 1987, the likes of which India had never seen before, as suave ladies, never exposed to such fashion, took time to sip juice in their traditional garb. Swishing saris with panniers and headdresses with ostrich feathers. Mannequins twirling silver walking sticks and sequinned sheers. Blue make-up and carmine shadows stunning catwalks. India saw with Zandra Rhodes, for the first time, its emerging fashion platforms! The initial shock of Zandra's innovative take on Indian fashion gave way to a wave of new-found design techniques that infiltrated the Indian fashion industry and helped kick-start the imaginative use of garments once known for their simplicity and traditional styling.

T for tents and Textile Museum

New concepts for Indian tents were high on my design agenda at around the time of the Hanover Expo, but I needed to configure one that could be a modular *Jugaar*, improvised for a more asymmetrical expansion. So, Zandra's carpet, made by Vorwerk in Germany, helped us pay for a complement of handmade props that we could put onto it. The rambling tent, capable of an infinite permutation of forms, happened and was displayed at the show – appliquéd, embroidered and structured using bamboo supports covered in

raw silk. Zandra worked day and night in extreme conditions in an ashram in South India, hours away from any proper hotel and amenities, to complete my installation.

Over the decades, I have watched Zandra carrying large garment bags on planes, negotiating frequent-flyer miles with genuine charm and chutzpah; storing trunks everywhere; and taking her growing asset of collections, drawings and patterns here, there, and everywhere. Moving this trove from her St Stephen's Gardens home in the early 2000s and making a museum in London's Bermondsey (then considered the proverbial 'back of beyond') was a courageous and visionary move. Finally, her legacy has a promise of a home for posterity at the Fashion and Textile Museum.

U for Udaipur

An Indian city with magical palaces in lakes, where Zandra and I started an adventure one Christmas that took us on to Ajmer and Pushkar, inspiring Zandra every day. Her sketchbook celebrated intricate inlays, trellis shadows, veiled women and bejewelled camels.

V for Vrindavan and the festival of colour

We celebrated the Hindu festival of colours, Holi, in the city of Mathura, where the blue god Krishna was born, leaving some of us sprayed with pink colour and looking a bit like Zandra! The queen of colour looks very much at home in this medieval town, to which we would follow Robyn Beeche, who had retired to an ashram to record the holy Hindu festivals and, in particular, this one, where child dancers dressed as gods were buried in rose petals.

Model in a Zandra Rhodes sari with feather headdress, cane and panniers, backstage at Rhodes's 1987 fashion show in Bombay (now Mumbai), India. Photo: Swapan Mukherjee.

W for woodcarving

The Papansami ashram near Trichy, created by an enigmatic swami, was making a valiant effort to revive time-honoured skills in the late 1990s, when we visited. The ancient swami took to Zandra, and her witty furniture and screens were carved for the Hanover display by dexterous carvers, who may have been bored of making ornate temple doorways and staircases for the homes of the newly rich wanting to live like film stars in a set.

X for Xandra

The name Zandra's mother was originally going to give her – spelt with an 'X', which was changed to a 'Z', as her grandmother said no one would be able to pronounce it.

Y for yellow! And yes!

Yellow is another magical colour – it complements Z's pink hair! Also, it is the colour of turmeric and the marigold-flower necklaces placed around her neck every time she visits! Zandra's never-failing ability to say 'Yes!' leads to innovation and sparks creativity.

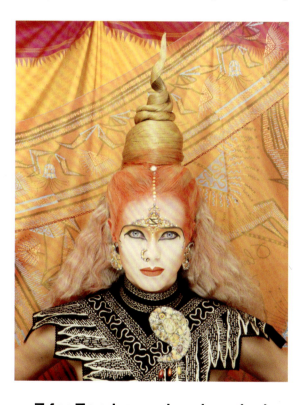

Z for Zandra, zari and zardozi

In her travels across India with me, Zandra was introduced to zardozi and zari work, two important techniques in Indian textile design. Zardozi, an artful embroidery technique, uses fine-metal wire or thread in gold and silver (or synthetic wires with copper coatings for cost-efficient applications) to create patterns of embellishment on silky fabrics such as velvet, satin and raw silks. Zari is a weaving technique making use of metallic threads. Through

her visits to India, Zandra started designing garments using such techniques. Her magical textile creations, originally conceived as prints, were interpreted to create wonderful beaded tunics and trousers, evening jackets and ball gowns. After 50 years, Z is also for zooming ahead and not stopping! Happy anniversary Zandra, and many more years before some well-deserved 'zzzz'.

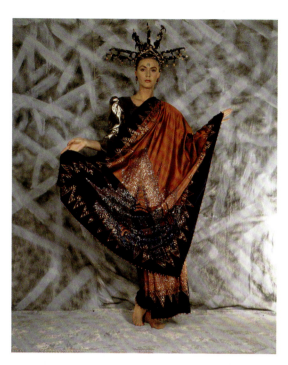

top Hand-beaded 'Manhattan' sari with headdress and gold *choli*, backstage at Rhodes's sari fashion show in India, December 1987. Photo: Robyn Beeche.
bottom The 'Holey Sari', backstage at Rhodes's sari fashion show in India, December 1987. Photo: Swapan Mukherjee.

Model posing for the 1983 Zandra Rhodes poster. Make-up: Richard Sharah. Photo: Greg Barrett.

As the 1990s ushered in a new era of fashion, Rhodes's work reflected these changes. Devoré velvets, hand-painted fabrics and bias-cut slip dresses were features of the designs produced during this decade, which included the beginning of some of her most imaginative projects: designing costumes and stage sets for opera.

Helena Christensen wearing a Zandra Rhodes silk chiffon shift, hand-beaded with diamanté 'Vogue' chains. British *Vogue*, June 1991. Photo: Patrick Demarchelier / Vogue © The Condé Nast Publications Ltd. This dress is now the property of the Fashion Museum, Bath.

1990–1999

this page and opposite (detail)
Spring/Summer 1990, 'Zandra Goes to Hollywood' collection. Rainbow silk chiffon knee-length dress with rolled chiffon embellished with pearls and topstitching at the shoulders, layered sleeves and skirt with pearl accents and trim, printed with 'Lace Mountain' design and a pearl trim, style 90/4. Kindly loaned by Mindy Aisen.

this page (detail) and opposite
Autumn/Winter 1990, 'Temples and Lotuses' collection. Discharge-printed black velvet knee-length dress, printed with 'Magic Carpet Border' design, style 90/628.

pp. 134–5
left Joanna Thomas wearing a raw silk mini dress with Zandra Rhodes printed tights from the 1991 'Flower Power' collection at a private photo shoot. Photo: Christopher Bissell.
right Spring/Summer 1991, 'Flower Power' collection. Close-up: Raw silk mini dress embellished with appliqué flowers made from ribbon, rope and wooden and metal beads, style 91/598.

this page
Autumn/Winter 1991, 'Celestial Bodies' collection. Three-colour
discharge-printed velvet, printed with 'Mr Man' design, with hand-
embroidered and metal-beaded buttons with metallic ribbon,
style 91/767.

opposite
Models in discharge-printed velvet jacket, printed with 'Byzantine
Swirl' design, worn with flowing silk chiffon trousers printed with
'Indian Border Stripe' design (left), and discharge-printed velvet
oversize jacket, hand-embroidered trim, worn with 'Mr Man' design
printed tights (right), from the 'Celestial Bodies' collection, backstage
at the Autumn/Winter 1991 fashion show. Photo: Robyn Beeche.

this page
Spring/Summer 1992,
'Cinderella Dreams in Colour'
collection. Crêpe de Chine
Italian silk scarf dress,
discharge printed with 'Lady
in Floral Frame' design, style
92/533.

opposite
Models in crêpe de Chine
printed mini dresses from
the 'Cinderella Dreams in
Colour' collection, backstage
at the Spring/Summer 1992
fashion show.
Photo: Jill Green.

this page and opposite
Autumn/Winter 1992, 'Pretty Woman' collection. Hand-embroidered, boned silk georgette bodice with silk organza skirt printed with 'Continuous Bows Squares' design, with a nylon net underskirt, style 92/636.

this page and opposite (detail)
Autumn/Winter 1992, 'Pretty Woman' collection. Short dress
with gold metallic lace and silk chiffon over-drape printed with
'Lace Carnation' design and attached at the bust, style 92/576.

this page and opposite *(detail)*
Spring/Summer 1999, 'Luxurious
Satin and Velvet' collection. Silk
and acetate satin devoré top and
matching trousers printed with
'Lace Manhattan' design, styles
99/179 (top) and 99/99 (trousers).

above
Detail of 'Floral Explosion Square' design from
the Autumn/Winter 1999 'Floral Explosion' collection.

opposite
Autumn/Winter 1999, 'Floral Explosion' collection. Devoré velvet
and silk evening gown with a pearl-beaded, low-draped back
neckline, floor-length with train, style 20/141.

146   ZANDRA RHODES: 50 FABULOUS YEARS IN FASHION

Geschi Fengler in a Zandra Rhodes quilted satin kaftan.
British *Vogue*, January 1970. Photo: Clive Arrowsmith / Vogue
© The Condé Nast Publications Ltd.

opposite, above
The Queen of the Night in *The Magic Flute* at San Diego Opera.
Photo: Ken Howard. Photo courtesy of San Diego Opera.
   opposite, below
Rhodes's sketch of *The Magic Flute*'s Queen of the Night.

ZANDRA RHODES BRINGS FASHION TO OPERA

Helena Matheopoulos

I first became aware of Zandra Rhodes in 1969 through the pages of British *Vogue*, my fashion bible – visually stunning and brilliantly erudite at the time, under the late Beatrix Miller, and almost as inspirational as Diana Vreeland's US edition, eagerly awaited at the beginning of each month.

I vividly remember the November day, the specific moment even, when, having prepared my ritual afternoon tea from Fortnum & Mason, I settled down in the unique armchair in my studio flat opposite London's Victoria and Albert Museum to peruse the pages of the freshly bought, new edition of *Vogue*. Then wham! Facing me was a four-page feature titled 'Fantastical Clothes by Zandra Rhodes: Fortnum & Mason's own Gipsy', illustrated with the most phantasmagorical clothes anyone had ever seen to date! Two pages of a mainly Spanish-yellow, satin gypsy dress and a Renaissance-style tunic, both in typical Zandra squiggly prints, and two pages of a yellow felt opera coat and an ethereal turquoise and Nile green printed chiffon kaftan.

That was it. Love at first glimpse! There and then I decided that if I could not have the gypsy dress (priced at £150 – a fortune in those days, when Bazaar and Biba dresses were around £10 or so), I would rather die.

Fast forward – a dash to F&M, where the clothes were brilliantly displayed in four windows entirely devoted to them. The opera coat and the kaftan were bought by Irene Worth and worn at the January 1970 British premiere of Edward Albee's *Tiny Alice*. The gypsy dress was bought by me, my having coaxed my mother into believing it would do as both a Christmas and a birthday present for the year! Wearing it made me feel on top of the world – tantamount to a transfusion of adrenaline and superhuman confidence! I remember even wearing it out to a Sunday lunch, with amazed people in the street probably assuming I had not gone home for the night. It was a supremely happy dress. Only nice things happened whenever I wore it and it opened many doors because it made me appear much more important than I was! This was also the start of my life-long friendship with Zandra, with many more clothes along the way.

Zandra has always been the most 'theatrical' of fashion designers. Bursting onto the London scene in the late 1960s, she took it by storm and set the tone for what was to follow for more than a decade, turning fashion into costume and transforming her environment into pure theatre. Zandra soon became as famous for her own unique appearance as for her psychedelic creations. Long before the punk movement was even heard of, she was painting her cheeks and hair royal blue or emerald green, before finally settling on her trademark fuchsia. In the mid-1970s, when the punk look eventually took hold, she brought it into the drawing room with her silk jersey tops complete with strategically placed slits and safety pins (this was nearly two decades before Gianni Versace's 'safety pin' dress was famously sported by Elizabeth Hurley). Yet, amazingly, for such an obviously theatrical designer, it was not until 2001 that she was asked to design costumes for the opera.

As it turned out, it was Zandra's home away from home in San Diego, California, that provided the setting for this invitation to the stage. Ian Campbell, the adventurous former general director of San Diego Opera, was well acquainted with her fashion designs – her particular love of colour and way with fabric. When he discovered that she lived in the city for part of the year, the seed for a possible collaboration was sown. 'But it really germinated,' he notes, 'when I first visited her home for dinner, and was absolutely bowled over. The fabrics, the colours and taste throughout the house simply made my mind start playing with ideas for operatic designs. By the end of dinner, I knew I had to find a way to work with her.'[1]

When, soon afterwards, Campbell suggested that Zandra design the costumes for a forthcoming production of *The Magic Flute*, her reaction was modest. She pointed out that she had no experience of operatic design and didn't even know much about opera. She quickly warmed, however, to the opportunity of having a 'runway', a larger canvas on which to work than that provided by fashion. 'What prompted me to accept,' she says, 'was the fact that opera is so over the top, so exotic! Until I came to live in San Diego I had hardly ever visited an opera house. But after accepting the assignment, it became quite an obsession, and now I love it and listen to it all the time, especially when trying to think my way into specific scenes and how they should look.'[2]

Of the process of designing for the opera (while creating actual designs, she says she tends to listen to the BBC's Radio 4, because she likes 'things going into my brain as I work'), she notes: 'I suppose I felt that the experience was really like doing a very, very exotic dress show, where the clothes are not there *per se*, but [exist] in order to say something specific about the various characters.' In common with most couturiers who have designed for the opera, Zandra notes that this is the fundamental difference between fashion and costume design. Naturally, it is also a totally different discipline from the technical point of view, as Zandra explains:

> In real-life clothes, you have to focus on detail, whereas on stage you have to make broad-brush statements because you're not going to be seeing those costumes at close quarters. So you've got to think, 'Is this or that costume going to be impressive enough from a distance?' Costumes also have to be quite practical, which places some restrictions on the sorts of materials you can use as a stage costumier. The singers have to be able to move around without being too hot, because the act of singing produces terrific body heat. Funnily enough, that's something costume designers don't always take into account.

As soon as Zandra accepted Campbell's offer, she committed herself to learning about *The Magic Flute*. According to Campbell, she had absolutely no conditions 'other than for us to recognise that, as her experience of stage design was minimal, we would need to teach her a few tricks.' The director Michael Hampe would explain the meaning of certain scenes and what each of the characters stood for, and then Zandra would come up with an appropriate costume. For this production, he had already decided that the

this page, top to bottom
Tamino with the magic animals in *The Magic Flute* at Seattle Opera. Photo: Rozarii Lynch, photo courtesy of Seattle Opera; Monostatos and the guards in *The Magic Flute*. Photo: Jacob Lewis, photo courtesy of Seattle Opera; Rhodes's sketch of *The Magic Flute*'s Monostatos.
opposite, top to bottom
Rhodes's sketch of the dancer with horse head for Bizet's *Pearl Fishers*; the dancer with horse head with 'the people' in Bizet's *Pearl Fishers* at Tulsa Opera. Photo: Shane Bevel Photography, photo courtesy of Tulsa Opera; Rhodes's sketch of Leila for Bizet's *Pearl Fishers*; Leila in Bizet's *Pearl Fishers*. Photo: Ken Howard, photo courtesy of San Diego Opera.

1 Ian Campbell in conversation with the author in 2009 and 2010. All subsequent quotations from Campbell date from this conversation.
2 Zandra Rhodes in conversation with the author in 2009 and 2010. All subsequent quotations from Rhodes date from this conversation.

Queen of the Night should descend to the stage riding on the moon. Zandra recalls the process of designing her costume:

> I said that if her cloak was meant to be the night sky, then let's make it look like the night sky. I suggested that it seemed logical to give her a cloak that unfolds as the night descends onto the stage and that the way to achieve this effect was by lowering a curtain made to look like a cloak. It was very cleverly done. In fact, we had to have two cloaks, two separate pieces of scenery: one that came up to the bottom of the cradle onto which she was strapped – a platform shaped like the moon, which was lowered from a height of about 40 feet – and another behind her that unfolded gradually, timed so that her cloak appeared to cover the entire stage, which turned into the night sky as she descended in her moon-shaped cradle. This was pure invention – unlike the yellow robes worn by the priests, which were a man's version of a jacket in my fashion collection!

With the exception of the spectacular stuffed animals, which were fabricated in London – among them a crocodile, a hippopotamus covered in mirrors and pearls, pink fluorescent monkeys that glowed in the dark, two griffins, eight-foot-tall lions with open jaws, and dragons that had 40 people under them – all of the costumes were made in San Diego. The budget was $250,000 for the sets and $200,000 for the costumes. Zandra particularly enjoyed designing for the chorus, 'who were all sizes'. She wanted the characters to belong to no country in particular, so dressed them 'to look vaguely golden, with some bits of my prints, plus fabrics from the nearby small towns on the Mexican border and some from a pile of old ethnic cushions that were applied onto a wrap . . . all sorts of mad things such as these.'

From the moment Zandra's involvement in the production was announced, there was immense interest and excitement. Some of the designs were previewed at the Museum of Contemporary Art in nearby La Jolla (now the Museum of Contemporary Art San Diego), and Campbell still remembers the extraordinary 'buzz' before the opening. Once the production was finally staged, the costumes were praised in the press and adored by the public, and 'such was the affection of the first-night audience for Zandra – a well-established figure in San Diego – that all three thousand opera-goers wore boas made of pink feathers in recognition of her signature colour – and hair'. The production in due course received accolades including an award for Best Live Theatrical Styling in the annual Hollywood Make-Up Artists and Hair Stylist Guild Awards in February 2002.

On the strength of her success, Zandra was invited to design both costumes and sets for the San Diego Opera production of Georges Bizet's *The Pearl Fishers* in 2004. Designing both elements was an altogether new departure, and Rhodes felt enormously excited and challenged by the project. The director of the production was Andrew Sinclair, a staff director at the Royal Opera House, London. He admits that he initially had some misgivings about the proposed collaboration:

> I was introduced to Zandra Rhodes by Ian Campbell, who thought we might be a good team. I have to confess I was slightly nervous. Of course I knew of Zandra and her work, but from a director's point of view, half of the contribution

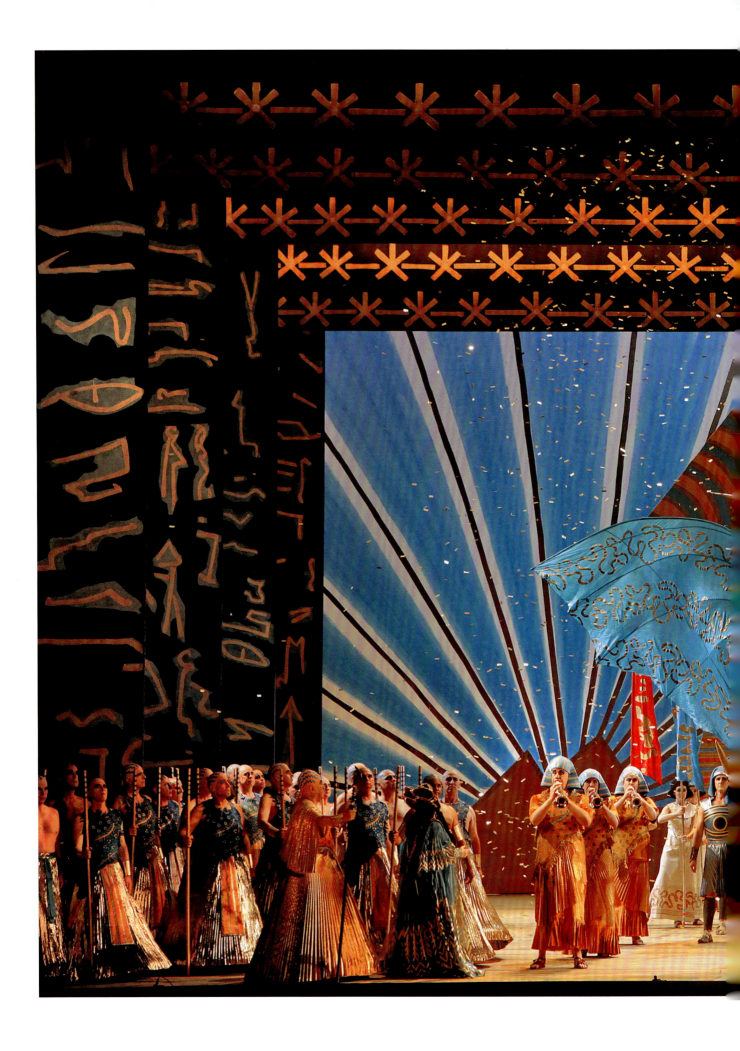

ZANDRA RHODES BRINGS FASHION TO OPERA

to a production comes from the designer – not just in what
a production looks like, but in what it says about the piece,
the characters and the director's dramatic approach. So
this would mean going into unknown territory for me with a
first-time set designer and second-time costume designer.[3]

One of Ian Campbell's main reasons for involving Rhodes was the
fact that the opera is set in Sri Lanka. He felt that the South Asian
motifs running through the piece would be a stimulating fit for her
vibrant imagination. 'The first sketches confirmed that my instinct
was right. Her flair for fabric and colour made it appear suitably
exotic, while her innate taste ensured that this wasn't going to
be a vulgar realisation.' Campbell realised that Zandra would, of
course, require some technical support to develop her ideas. 'But
to have her mind's eye on all aspects of the opera's visual side
would ensure an integrated whole, and a colour palette that would
blend costumes and sets harmoniously.'

Another factor in favour of the collaboration was Campbell's
confidence that Rhodes could work within the confines of this
budget – this time $300,000 for sets and $165,000 for the costumes. Neither he nor the director wanted an expensive, 'over the
top' staging. The production was also intended to travel to other
theatres across the US and abroad, so a certain degree of flexibil-
ity was required. Campbell and Sinclair asked for a set painted on
soft cloth so that it could be adjusted to suit the various venues to
which it would travel. 'So most of the set was stretched-out canvas,'
explains Rhodes, 'which enabled it to adapt to the size of different
stages. If the stage in question was two metres smaller on each
side, then the canvas could just be rolled up.'

Rhodes realised that realistic drawings were not what the team
at San Diego expected from her. 'If they wanted that, they could
have gone to someone within the operatic circuit. I think they came
to me for the Zandra Rhodes imagination and vision of things. As
Ian pointed out to me, Bizet had never been to Sri Lanka – or to
Spain for his *Carmen*, for that matter. He'd never seen the place.
Originally the story was going to be set in Mexico, which he hadn't
seen either! So the whole thing is about imagination, about Zandra
Rhodes's take on the story, i.e., something exotic.' 'In the end it
boiled down to what we wanted to say about the piece,' adds
Andrew Sinclair, 'which is a difficult one for a director: beautiful
music, weak libretto. The music is lush and exotic, but there is also
a tribal, almost primitive element to the story. To try and convey
this, I had already decided there would be more dance in this
production than just the set pieces. So we needed a clear stage
for dance, and we needed a production that would be attractive for
other companies to hire. It was important that we presented what
Zandra could bring to the piece – a wonderful sense of colour,
texture and fabric. So in the end the set design was quite easy.'

Zandra recalls that she 'loved every minute' of the process. As
she recalls: 'The workshop of the technical department was in a
dilapidated building in a rough downtown area, where they build
scenery and props for theatres all over America.' In this workshop
she learned some of the technicalities of stage design, such as the
fact that it has to be *bold*. The workshop equally adored working
with Rhodes, who, according to Ian Campbell, 'taught as much as

3 Andrew Sinclair in conversation with the author in 2009 and 2010.
All subsequent quotations from Sinclair date from this conversation.

she learned, leaving the team with some new ideas they will utilise for years to come, and it was done with such affection and humour that no one could ask for more.' Rhodes recalls an instance of applying this kind of ingenuity to a staging problem:

> In the opening scene, the action takes place on a sunny, sandy beach; then a storm has taken place, so the set is grey and dreary, and the singers are standing and moving on rain puddles. We devised a floor made of cloth, which at the beginning had to be hammered down. For the opening scene, on the sunny beach, a yellow layer went on top of that. Simple! So, when, halfway through the opera, you have the storm, all you needed to do was remove the yellow layer and, at a stroke, you had the setting for the second half.

For the costumes, Rhodes used cheap polyester saris, which she got at a market just outside Los Angeles. She brought them back to her studio in London, where she printed over them and, as she puts it, 'Zandra-fied' them. After a trip to India, she went back to San Diego and worked on the wigs and make-up, so that they could be made to look as authentically South Asian as possible. The entire work is so cleverly packaged that it has travelled to cities all over North America, including Michigan, San Francisco, Miami, Denver, Minneapolis and Montreal.

By the time Zandra came to design her third opera, *Aida*, a co-production with the Houston Grand Opera (2007), English National Opera and San Francisco Grand Opera (2011), she had discovered that 'you have to spar a little with each director, and see how you can come to a solution that fulfils both [of] your visions, although the overall concept of the production is always theirs.' Jo Davies, who directed all three stagings, explains that the project was put together by John Berry, artistic director at the ENO, and Anthony Freud, general director at Houston:

> [They] were looking for a co-production of *Aida* that would be planned very much around Zandra. This is the other way round from the usual process of planning a production, when the director usually chooses his designing team. They asked me if I could meet Zandra and see if we can deliver such an *Aida*. So we met in London and the images themselves were fantastic, so I said yes right away. The spirit of her designs was very much in keeping with what Verdi wanted. In his notes, he asked for colours that are bright and rich and splendid. He wanted a vibrancy and exoticism that are perfectly matched with Zandra's designs.[4]

Verdi's highly 'exotic' opera, *Aida*, which premiered at the Cairo Opera in 1871, is ideally suited to a large stage, but it also contains an intense, intimate drama, which takes place between the four main characters. Aida, slave of the Pharaoh's daughter, Princess Amneris, is herself an Ethiopian princess and daughter of the vanquished Ethiopian king Amonasro. She shares her mistress's passion for the young Egyptian army commander Radames (who is in turn in love with Aida but is chosen to lead the Egyptian army's attack on her country). The danger that the larger-than-life background to the opera might be allowed to overshadow the inner drama must be carefully averted. Zandra's work reflected the director's concept:

> I took a very colourful view of Egypt, based on some of my personal sketches, done back in 1985, and on some of Napoleon's Egyptian campaign etchings – translated into very bright colours: turquoise, gold, ultramarine, orange. I visualise Aida herself as smouldering. She must exude sexuality. She must look 'civilised' and, at the same time, 'ethnic'. I based her make-up on Tuareg faces – an ethnic touch, so that she doesn't look Egyptian. Princess Amneris is tortured and spoilt. She must have regal presence, and my job is to make the diva feel and act *thinner*! Radames is ambitious and conscious of being head of the Egyptian army. He must look handsome – whatever his build – and *believable*. Amonasro, the warrior king of Ethiopia and Aida's father, has to look handsome and, like her, 'ethnic'. I printed my African zebra print on brown suede to hang across his body, and used rough paintwork on ethnic-style fabric for trousers, etc.

Zandra's initial concept was that, as in original Egyptian tomb paintings and papyri, the women would go bare-breasted.

> My idea was that they would wear flesh-coloured body stockings tightly stretched so that you wouldn't get any wrinkling. This is quite common practice, because most opera singers don't like having their arms bare, so they usually wear a transparent fabric over them, as do most people in show business, including ice skaters. The fabric would make the cast look as if they were naked, with their armlets and bracelets made of a stick-on fabric that looks like brocade. My idea was to have those flesh-coloured body stockings and then paint the nipples and the accessories on. There was no way I would have them go around stark naked . . . but the people at Houston said that because Texas was part of the Bible Belt, they couldn't envisage them even *looking* naked on the stage. So I had to raise the bodysuits to cover their breasts. This was a compromise . . . The materials were polyester because it pleats beautifully, the pleats never come out, and pleated polyester is then washable. The collars were beautifully made – of leather and raised acrylics.

Jo Davies was more than satisfied with the costumes Rhodes had produced on her budget of $250,000 for sets and costumes, with an additional $50,000 for props. While Zandra was rehearsing in Houston, Anthony Freud mentioned that he could imagine her doing a production of *Turandot*. Would she like to have a go at Giacomo Puccini's 'Chinese' opera, and does she have any unfulfilled dreams as far as the operatic stage is concerned? 'Opera as an art form is like the sky's limit,' she replies. 'You can't go any higher or any better than that. I hope that some director, somewhere, will think of me and propose some future collaboration. Then I'll listen to the music, imagine it in visual terms, and produce my own version of what it should look like!'

4 Jo Davies in conversation with the author in 2010. All subsequent quotations from Davies date from this conversation.

Whilst continuing to produce new prints and collections, Rhodes explored digital printing in these years, alongside the trademark hand-printed textiles. This decade saw the development of a major undertaking on the part of the designer: the formation of the Fashion and Textile Museum in London.

Gabriella Wilde wearing a Zandra Rhodes top from the Spring/Summer
2004 'Pop' collection. *Tatler*, January 2004.
Photo: Yu-Kuang Chou / Tatler © The Condé Nast Publications Ltd.

2000–2009

this page
Autumn/Winter 2005, 'Flowers, Flounces and Frills' collection. Silk chiffon gown printed with 'Shamrock Explosion' design, with chiffon frill accents on the skirt flowing down to the train, style 05/124. Kindly loaned by Jeanne Jones.

opposite
Tatiana Slepova wearing a silk chiffon gown from the 'Flowers, Flounces and Frills' collection, backstage at the 2018 'Go Red for Women' fashion show. Photo: Tim Vechik.

this page
Autumn/Winter 2005, 'Flowers,
Flounces and Frills' collection.
Silk chiffon patchwork kaftan
printed with 'Fantastic Flower
Garden', 'Mad Crochet Frill',
'Manhattan', 'Pop Starry Frill',
'Pattern Pieces', 'Torn Shell',
'Feather' and 'Triangle' designs,
style 05/160.
    opposite
Silk chiffon kaftan from the
'Flowers, Flounces and Frills'
collection, backstage at the
Spring/Summer 2007 catwalk,
London Fashion Week.
Photo: Morgan O'Donovan.

pp. 166–67
Spring/Summer 2008, 'Sparkling Sequin' collection (detail, left). Metallic silk chiffon, printed with 'Sparkling Sequin' design, accented with silver metallic sequins on the bodice and hem and silver metallic panel on the bodice, style 08/30.

this page and opposite
Spring/Summer 2009, 'Dandelion' collection. Silk organza mini dress, constructed from 52 individual fabric circles printed with silver and gold 'Chinese Water Circles' designs, separately attached, with a deep laced-up neckline, style 09/02.

Cynthia Korman in a printed chiffon scarf by Zandra Rhodes and fur
coat by Christian Dior, hair by Ara Gallant, New York, 30 June 1969.
Photo: Richard Avedon © The Richard Avedon Foundation.

THE MARK AND THE ART:
ON THE PATTERNS OF ZANDRA RHODES

Mary Schoeser

In 1984, when writing the introduction to *The Art of Zandra Rhodes*, Dame Zandra Rhodes explained why she wanted to chart the stories behind her designs: 'They are not produced lightly and flippantly, but evolve through an interpretation of my surroundings, seen in my own special way. I feel that one of the major contributions to the world of fashion I have been able to make is my originality of textile print design and the way I have allowed the textiles to influence the garment shapes.' Now celebrating 50 years since her first public collection – and five more since Heal's produced one of her Royal College of Art (RCA) degree show screen-printed textiles, which they called 'Top Brass' – it is even more evident that no British fashion designer has surpassed her ability to prove the importance of patterned fashion fabrics as an inspirational springboard for garment shapes.

As a consistent proponent of pattern-driven garment design, both Rhodes's fashions and the designer herself have been the subject of many articles and essays, as well as three other monographs. However, despite her own belief that 'what I do is as valid as fine art',[1] there has been very little analysis of the artistic context of her patterns, as opposed to the thought processes behind their creation or their final uses. To redress this balance, one can begin by comparing her work to that of Arts and Crafts pioneer William Morris, the author of equally distinctive and influential design concepts. Although there is no similarity between the patterns of the two, Rhodes's work nevertheless satisfies the guidelines set out in an 1881 lecture by Morris and posthumously published in *Some Hints on Pattern Designing* (1899):

> In recurring patterns, at least, the noblest are those where one thing grows visibly and necessarily from another. Take heed in this growth that each member of it be strong and crisp, that the lines do not get thready or flabby or too far from their stock to sprout firmly and vigorously.[2]

Compare Morris's 'strong and crisp' lines that 'sprout firmly and vigorously' to the distinctive Rhodes squiggle and stroke: free yet firm, bold and energetic. Yet unlike Morris – or the vast majority of other creators of printed textiles – Rhodes does not specialise in traditionally repeating designs, but often treats her cloth as a canvas with a directional emphasis. Today it may seem unsurprising, then, that her signature marks from the beginning have drawn comparisons with other artists, rather than other pattern designers. When she was 'discovered' in 1969 by Diana Vreeland, then the influential editor of American *Vogue*, the first designs to be featured under her own name included a chiffon scarf described as 'fascinating, like a [René] Magritte painting'.[3]

The timing of Vreeland's remark is significant, occurring as it did at a heated moment amid the visual, verbal and occasionally physical outbursts characteristic of the New York art scene in the late 1960s. There were bitter exchanges between conservative art critics such as Clement Greenberg (aged 60 in 1969), whose aim was to preserve a Modernist hierarchy privileging abstract, self-critical easel painters, and those artists who wished to free themselves from the seemingly rigid expectations of reviewers and museum professionals. The situation is captured by Willem de Kooning's fear that he would become a 'sausage' stamped 'Museum of Modern Art', as described by Lane Slate in 1963:

> Just as the art world had packed and stamped the Willem de Kooning sausage, by the time of de Kooning's retrospective in 1968 it had also made sausage out of abstract expressionism as a whole . . . Already in 1965 when the Los Angeles County Museum of Art presented *New York School: The First Generation, 15 Artists,* a frustrated [Barnett] Newman felt that 'the attitude toward the show by those who organised it [was] as if we were all dead' and that 'the doctors of art history are not so much doctoring history as they are hoping that the patient will disappear'.[4]

In this complex, contested space, Susan Sontag, the subject of an Andy Warhol Screen Test in 1964, was simultaneously arguing that one should focus on the materiality of art rather than dry, 'progressive' interpretations of it. By this time, Rhodes had a keen eye for those in sympathy with Sontag, recalling 'I saw the Mark Rothko at the Whitechapel [Gallery, in London] around 1961. My work in college was influenced by [Roy] Lichtenstein, Warhol and [David] Hockney.'[5] Meanwhile Robert Motherwell, the intellectual leader of the New York School, now more commonly known as Abstract Expressionism (with which Rothko was associated), was in direct conflict with Greenberg and instead positioning automatism and

---

1   Zandra Rhodes in correspondence with the author, 27 August 2018.

2   William Morris, *Some Hints on Pattern Designing*, London: Longmans, 1899, p. 36.

3   'Vogue's own boutique of suggestions, finds and observations', American *Vogue*, vol. 153, issue 10, 1 June 1969, p. 158. Other comments include: 'our heroine wraps her head in a chiffon scarf . . . and what better Surrealist way to show off a beautiful printed scarf of black, pink, blue on white chiffon . . . designed and sold by the Fulham Road Clothes Shop, 160 Fulham Road . . . it goes with an "interior" robe . . . large and loose, same print, $20 [and] an extra long, flow-y scarf, $12.' I'm indebted to Dilys Blum for this full reference.

4   Barnett Newman, 'Interview with Lane Slate' [1963], cited in Valerie Hellstein, 'De Kooning's Embodied Vision and Abstract Expressionism in the 1960s', in Valerie Hellstein (ed.), *In Focus:* Women Singing II *1966 by Willem de Kooning*, Tate Research Publications, 2017, www.tate.org.uk/research/publications/in-focus/women-singing-ii/de-koonings-embodied-vision (accessed 22 August 2018).

5   This and all unattributed statements are Zandra Rhodes in conversation with the author, 3 August 2018.

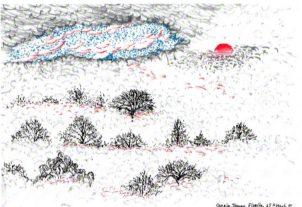

psychoanalysis as key means of both making and understanding art. Although Greenberg had changed his views by the time of Motherwell's death in 1991, it is clear that Motherwell's participation in making multiples, or series, was deemed too commercial by Greenberg at the time, reducing art to the decorative. Worse, no doubt, was the fact that Motherwell and his third wife, Helen Frankenthaler, had in 1963 each allowed the latter's sister, Gloria F. Ross, to produce a hand-hooked, wool-on-canvas, one-off rendition of one of their paintings. Motherwell's *tapis* (literally, 'carpet') was after *Elegy to the Spanish Republic, No. 78*, and by the time Ross commissioned the Dovecot Studios in Edinburgh to make seven hand-woven Motherwell tapestries (1970–76), these were based on the 116th in his *Elegy* series.[6]

Events such as Valerie Solanas's mid-1968 attempt on the life of Andy Warhol brought notoriety to self-proclaimed feminist protest, as well as Pop Art in general and Warhol's Factory in particular. Having emerged in the 1950s, Pop Art had succeeded by the 1960s in its aim of undermining elitist art institutions by adopting commercial imagery and production techniques, such as screen-printing. Rhodes was aware of this movement, not least because in England the principal proponents were members of the Independent Group, convened in 1952. Among the young artists involved were Nigel Henderson and Eduardo Paolozzi, who established Hammer Prints Ltd in 1954, designing fabrics, wallpaper, ceramics and homewares. Soon – and for another two decades – their textiles were being manufactured by Hull Traders, founded in 1957 by Tristram Hull to produce short runs of screen-printed furnishing fabrics. Creative direction until 1979 was provided by Shirley Craven, a 1959 RCA graduate soon renowned for her bold, abstract patterns. Entering the RCA not long afterwards, in 1961, Zandra admired Craven's work and might well have followed in her footsteps (Heal's furnishing fabric aside, her interiors work has included late-1960s designs produced by Sanderson and Angelo Donghia's company, Vice Versa; an extensive range of home furnishing items with Christopher Vane Percy in the 1970s, branded Zandra Rhodes Living; a 1987 collection for Osborne & Little; 1990s rug designs for Hill & Company and terrazzo collaborations with Australian artist David Humphries; and, of course, her own homes). Her choice of fashion, instead, as her principal artistic expression is the result of her love of the performative qualities of cloth: 'I would say that I am an artist who just went into textiles [because] I've always enjoyed the fact that you are putting pattern on a fabric and you are totally creating the mood of the whole thing by what you are doing to the fabric.' Favouring silk chiffon over other possibilities, although not limiting her cloths to one type only, she continues: 'So much of that is done by the textiles; you can just let the textile *do* something.'

Was it this intuitive engagement with cloth that Vreeland recognised and championed? Certainly, her choice of René Magritte as a comparison demonstrates her support for anti-establishment art.

top
Zandra Rhodes printed interior fabrics for Christopher Vane Percy, CVP Designs.

middle and bottom
Sketches by Rhodes of the sunrise in Tampa, Florida in March 1991 and of women in evening gowns.

6   For further information on the Gloria F. Ross Center for Tapestry Studies, see http://tapestrycenter.org/?page_id=10 (accessed 27 August 2018).

The last supper. Folk ceramic. Rancho la Puerta.

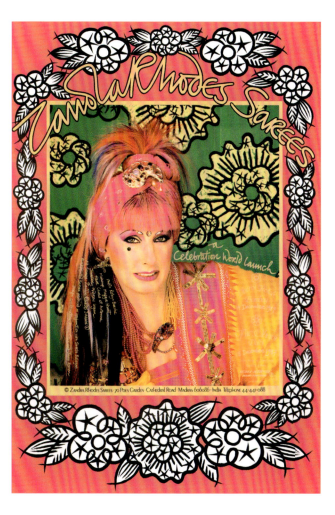

Magritte's idiosyncratic approach to Surrealism and his production of multiple copies of the same image had been criticised by 'elite' art critics, but after his death, this approach was once again being celebrated. Rhodes's approach aligns not only with Magritte's oeuvre and his concept of series, but also with the work of Warhol, Motherwell (and Paolozzi, whose *Whitworth Tapestry* was woven by the Dovecot Studios in 1967), and the many other artists who were engaging with textiles, as well as more generally countering the dismissal of the decorative and useful. Beyond that, Magritte's witty, dreamlike and thought-provoking images often incorporated the figure, for some time eschewed in 'high art' but essential to Zandra's artistic vision. Arguably, continued promotion in magazines such as *Vogue* into the 1970s made her garments the first widely seen examples of what has since been called Art-to-Wear.

Fast forward to Spring 2018, when an exhibition entitled *Textile, Print, and Form: A Lifetime of Magical Experimentation* was mounted at CAM, the contemporary art museum in Raleigh, North Carolina. Its director of exhibitions, Eric Gaard, argued the relevance of this exhibition thus: '[Zandra has] always approached her work as an artist and not a fashion designer . . . Her thinking transcends fashion. Her approach to process is really critical – she's still sketching every single day. She approaches all of her work as an artist would.'[7] One can't help but notice that the traditionalist's hierarchy remains in place despite the final compliment: fashion, it seems, still cannot be art. In a tangled trajectory, the designer herself, by contrast, can embody art, and there is no doubt that Rhodes's celebrity-artist status is unrivalled for its longevity. While praised with Thea Porter and Bill Gibb in 1975 for conjuring up 'very expensive, timeless and totally irrelevant dresses which could only be justified as art for art's sake', only Zandra of the three maintained a presence in the worlds of both print and fashion beyond the 1980s.[8] Asked about press attention, she said 'Yes, but mainly it is always about my personal life: how I live or whatever. It's hardly ever about the clothes!'

Given that Zandra has preserved hundreds of her bound, rice-paper-filled volumes, the aforementioned sketchbooks contain a broad range of imagery. From landscapes to architectural forms, whether a deft impression of a sunrise or a swiftly observed sculptural detail, each sketch is identifiable as being by Zandra Rhodes. The swift and sure stroke is always present. As an early postmodernist, she has embraced the breadth of art forms that today are gathered together under that label. Her ethereal squiggles contribute the essentially Surrealist 'dreaminess' that characterises so many garments, while patterns that reference objects are subtly subversive in their appropriation. Beginning in the 1970s, Zandra's study of Elizabethan pinked silks led to patterns composed in such a way as to highlight areas of slashing, a parallel to *décollage* (literally 'unstick' or 'lift off'), the practice of tearing through layers and other forms of seemingly random removals adopted in mid-century France and Germany, leading not only to Pop Art but also to

above
Rhodes's sketch of a Mexican ceramic interpretation of the Last Supper, in Rancho la Puerta, Mexico in the late 1990s.
below
Rhodes on her 1987 sari poster. Hair: Chris at Antenna. Make-up: Maggie Hunt. Jewellery: Andrew Logan. Photo: Robyn Beeche.

7   Jennifer Bringle, 'Dame Zandra Rhodes' garments are works of art', Triangle Today, www.triangletoday.com/performing-visual-arts-raleigh/dame-zandra-rhodes-garments-are-works-of-art-23710 (accessed 22 August 2018).
8   Alison Adburgham, *Liberty's: A Biography of a Shop*, London, Allen & Unwin, 1975, p. 131.

'happenings'. Such precursors to performance art find a parallel in both the staging of Zandra's (then-unorthodox) early fashion shows and the jolting drama expressed by her 1977 elevation and beautification of the punk street style, as well as in the logical twenty-first-century outcome of these innovations, with Zandra becoming a designer of opera costumes. Mark-making is always present, so that even her externalised seams, as in the 1971 'dinosaur coat' (see p. 32), become outlining, defining chevrons, while the use of tears and beaded pins in her punk 'Conceptual Chic' collections can be seen to be positioned along lyrical lines that echo the movement of brushstrokes.

An equal partner to her hand is the brush she holds, one of the many Japanese Tombow watercolour pens that she has been using since 1971. Her adoption of this tool was groundbreaking, as explained by the influential educator Jo Ann C. Stabb (herself fluent in fashion illustration, having trained at the Tobé-Coburn School for Fashion Careers in New York, as well as completing an MA at the University of California, Los Angeles, before beginning her teaching career in 1968 at the University of California, Davis). On the impact of a 1970 American *Vogue* issue featuring the 'Indian Feathers' print, she recalls:

> [There were] feathers and wiggly, organic, amorphous, abstracted prints. She was a breath of fresh air. She would take a theme – squiggles, undulating lines – never configured to the shape of the garment, but very painterly, free forms. The drawing tool was 50 per cent of this freedom – very clear, wonderful sketches, the marks gave a permanent line that didn't smudge or drip like paint or other liquid media such as the India[n] ink we were all using for fashion illustrations. Her tools were important; she was drawing, a great artist. We still had tempera, paint over pencil, but the release from the ink was major. We embraced instead that soft nib, the flow of the media.[9]

After decades of showing Zandra's work to her own students, Stabb added, 'Any person teaching design would respond similarly.' *The Art of Zandra Rhodes* was to become a bible within North American art and design colleges after its publication in 1984, and such was demand that it was republished in 1995. Although only briefly a part-time teacher (at what was then known as Ravensbourne College of Art and Design, and from 2018, Ravensbourne University London), Zandra's own teaching experience grounds and informs the approach in the book, which she co-wrote with Anne Knight. Its clear and generous insights into her creative process not only showcase her own work, but also document the postmodernist ethos that opposes the formalities of the 'tasteful', instead embracing all cultures and subcultures, and all eras. Art textiles – that is, constructed textile forms, whether wall hangings or baskets – had already begun to reflect multicultural influences when the book

was published. However, the radical post-Pop and Op changes taking place in the creation of *printed* fabric design itself – whether for fashion or furnishing – were undoubtedly accelerated in the mid-1980s (when much of the world was entranced with the English 'country house' style and 'power-dressing' women) by the widespread exposure of students and practitioners to Zandra's pioneering perspective.

The venerated textile artist Rozanne Hawksley (also an RCA graduate) was, similarly, showing Zandra's work to the trainee art teachers who were her students at Manresa House (Battersea College of Education, now London South Bank University) from 1968 to 1978, as well as the art students gathered around her at Goldsmiths' College (now Goldsmiths, University of London) from 1980 to 1987. She did so because Zandra was 'something else – not just a textile designer. Like so many painters or sculptors, she has a response to events or places that is quite rare, showing an artist's eye. What emerges from her observation is an intuitive response and the guts, strength and determination to externalise it.'[10] At Goldsmiths, David Green – a fellow student of Zandra's at the RCA – ran the textile print and dye room from around 1965 until 1978, when Rozanne was a sabbatical-leave, post-graduate student there. An insight into his own artistic values can be found in his recent statement that 'drawing is not subservient to any other art form . . . the line is master of the whole story.'[11] Hawksley has vivid memories of his response to any student who said the Rhodes style was flippant or superficial: 'He would refer to the breadth of her work, her focused mind and eyes, and he would bellow "she *WORKS*, she does it *ALL*" to emphasise the importance of her attitude.'[12] Zandra herself knows this: 'The whole reason that you do things is because you believe in them, but it is still a struggle to get the whole world to follow behind and use the things! I find my career goes like this: one minute it is you really are up and then everyone wants you and then it goes down a bit and if you really are lucky it comes up again.'

Zandra need not worry. Among fashion designers, John Galliano, Christian Lacroix and Issey Miyake are just some of those who have acknowledged her influence. Stella McCartney has paid visual homage to Zandra's patterns, and Valentino requested new designs for their Spring/Summer 2017 collection. Jane Rapley OBE, Professor Emerita at Central Saint Martins (CSM, University of the Arts London) and the Dean of Fashion and Textiles who established CSM as the fashion-training powerhouse it is today, has reflected recently: 'I can't think of anyone since Sonia Delaunay and maybe Emilio Pucci who have made a sustained fashion business entirely based on print.' On the other hand, she continues, 'Zandra's business model has been used by the subsequent generation, such as Mary Katrantzou, Eley Kishimoto and, to a lesser extent, Alice Temperley.'[13] One distinction remains, however. Zandra's ranges are – with the exception of the digitally printed 'The Sketchbook' collection of Spring/Summer 2013 – still screen-printed by hand.

---

9   Jo Ann C. Stabb in conversation with the author, 20 July 2018.

10   Rozanne Hawksley in conversation with the author, 5 and 21 August 2018.

11   For further information on David Green, see https://reasonsuspended.wordpress.com (accessed 27 August 2018).

12   Rozanne Hawksley in conversation with the author, 5 and 21 August 2018.

13   Jane Rapley in correspondence with the author, 21 August 2018.

The founding in 2003 of the Fashion and Textile Museum in London expresses Zandra's offering to up-and-coming designers: its vivid orange and pink exterior has made a positive mark on the neighbourhood of Bermondsey and contains spaces for directed learning as well as inspirational exhibitions. Tucked away are her workshops and screen-printing tables. She is still making marks, literally and conceptually.

Her approach to catwalk shows has also modified expectations across the industry (see pp. 56–61 for Anna Sui's response to a 1974 New York event). It is worth recording Zandra's own recollection of staging these every other year from 1972 onwards, first at the Roundhouse, London, and then, from 1977 until 1988, orchestrated as fantasy-themed spectaculars at the Pillar Hall, Olympia, in London's West Kensington:

> I remember these fondly, as they were a great gelling of many talents. It was always a privilege to work with such people as Derek Jarman, Patrick Libby and Ron Link who all helped choreograph, while Leonard and Trevor Sorbie devised intricate hairstyles, [and] Richard Sharah, Phyllis Cohen and Yvonne Gold created extraordinary visages to help create image campaigns, which Robyn Beeche then photographed. Phillip Treacy and Stephen Jones designed hats for me and Andrew Logan the co-ordinating jewellery.[14]

Adding her continued indebtedness to her design team and studio staff for helping to create the clothes, this generous – and genuine – statement belies the influence these events had, transforming Paris runway showings.

In addition, having visited India often and developed two collections as a result (in 1982 and 1985), she was invited again by the Indian government and escorted by the acclaimed scenographer, interior designer and art curator Rajeev Sethi, resulting in her 'Indian Sari' show being held in the Taj Bombay (Mumbai) and Taj Delhi in 1987. It was 'before India had proper dress shows. I did a dress show and I did panniers and walking sticks and ostrich feathers on their heads. I did *cholis* [short-sleeved bodices worn under saris]. With shoulder pads!' The Fashion Design Council of India (FDCI) was established in the following year and its first fashion show took place in 2000 in New Delhi, which has become the capital of Indian fashion. On her impact in this regard, Zandra reflects: 'Yes, it is funny how you make the mark. You don't know you're making that mark.'

One final mark must be mentioned. Throughout Zandra's 50 years in fashion, she has expressed a vision that has allowed others to find their own ways to oppose social and gender stereotypes. Her instantly recognisable, unorthodox personal style hides both outer and inner beauty. An equally talented painter–designer, Sarah Campbell, sums up Zandra thus: 'Neon hair, vibrant lipstick, magnificent jewellery, showstopping eyebrows – yes, that's Zandra as we all know her, an icon of her own style. But to me she has always been – first and foremost – an artist with and for textile.' This insider's observation goes on to provide a perfect final statement about Zandra's patterns:

> Zandra Rhodes has remained true to her paintings, using her observational sketches as the source for her textile designs, flowing from sketchbook to cloth via the print table – a direct visual journey. As a fashion designer, she has built garments around her love of surface pattern, the glory of colour and their happy marriage on a well-chosen cloth; her intimate knowledge and control of the processes ensure, and insist on, the integrated and faithful translation of her vision. A garment from ZR is pure Zandra from start to finish – despite the scissors![15]

14   Zandra Rhodes, 'The Eighties: What do I remember?', unpublished typescript from the Rhodes archive (accessed 25 September 1999).

15   Sarah Campbell in correspondence with the author, 22 August 2018.

In the present day, Rhodes's collections are still breaking new ground, with different materials and prints introduced; the designer also continues to interpret her archival works in modern and innovative ways. Her large and remarkable oeuvre inspires a new generation as she undertakes a series of collaborations, most notably with Valentino and Kurt Geiger.

Graysha Audren wearing a 'Frilly Square' midi dress from the 'Looking Back, Looking Forward' collection, backstage at the Zandra Rhodes Spring/ Summer 2019 presentation for London Fashion Week. Make-up: MAC. Photo: Bridie O'Sullivan.

2010–2019

opposite
Megan Deverson wearing a
satin mini dress from the 2012
'New Beginnings' collection.
Hat: Piers Atkinson.
Photo: Emma Hampson-Jones
and Luke Reynolds.
this page
Autumn/Winter 2012, 'New
Beginnings' collection. Satin
mini dress, digitally printed
with 'Jungle Trail' design,
style 12/83.

opposite
Jorden Alhashim in an ultrasuede ensemble, backstage at the 2018 'Go Red for Women' fashion show.
Photo: Tim Vechik.

this page
Autumn/Winter 2015, 'Lace Forest' collection. Ultrasuede jacket and matching trousers printed with metallic 'Egyptian Pleating with Shadow' design, styles 15/193 (jacket) and 15/199 (trousers).

this page and opposite
Spring/Summer 2016, 'Batik'
collection. Denim jacket and jeans
hand-painted with Zandra Rhodes
signature and signature motifs,
styles D16/83A (jacket) and
D16/82A (jeans). Kindly loaned
by Reena Horowitz.

opposite
Silk chiffon gown from the
'Songket Brocade' collection,
backstage at the Autumn/Winter
2016 catwalk show, London
Fashion Week.
Photo: Andrew Woffinden.
  this page
Autumn/Winter 2016, 'Songket
Brocade' collection. One-shoulder
evening gown with satin band,
with four layers of silk chiffon
circles; each layer is printed and
individually cut from the 'Knitted
Circle' design, style 16/157.

this page
Close-up: Autumn/Winter 2018, 'Party' collection. Sunray pleated shimmer satin jumpsuit with fan-pleated bodice, attached to three-quarter-length pleated trousers with a black tie that ties into a bow at the back, style 18/106.
opposite
Flora Miles wearing sangria shimmer satin from the Autumn/Winter 2019 'The Golden Hour' collection, style 18/106, backstage at the Zandra Rhodes Autumn/Winter 2019 presentation for London Fashion Week. Make-up: MAC. Earrings: Andrew Logan. Photo: Richard Dowker.

ZANDRA RHODES X VALENTINO: WHY PIERPAOLO CHOSE ZANDRA FOR HIS FIRST SOLO COLLECTION

Pierpaolo Piccioli

When I think of Zandra Rhodes I see a free spirit, a true artist, a brilliant and independent woman, who has always stood up for diversity. She played a fundamental role in a delicate moment of my life and I am grateful to have the opportunity to celebrate her extraordinary personality today.

In October 2016, after years of co-direction and decades of cooperation, I presented my first solo collection as the creative director of Maison Valentino. It was me in front of a blank page, and I wanted something that could express the change that I was living and that I needed to live. While questioning my aesthetic identity, I realised that I was trying to establish a connection with those artistic personalities who had lived through significant epochal transformations, because it is in such periods that free minds and spirits arise. In those little gaps in time, when history is moving forward, you need to break down walls.

I thought about Hieronymus Bosch and Zandra Rhodes – so distant in time but so close in the way they approached their time. They both represented what they were living with a different voice, a voice out of the choir, but still strongly connected to what they were witnessing. Zandra honoured me by reinterpreting Bosch's *The Garden of Earthly Delights* (1490–1500), the main informing motif of the collection. She had everything I was looking for: the freedom, the colour, the lightness, the punk culture – and all of that in her own individual way.

I still remember the emotion of watching her first sketches; I could not have asked for a more vibrant and unconventional vision. I was astonished by her talent for combining pictorial and pop symbols such as flames, hearts, lipsticks and thunderbolts, in shades of red and pink. It was unique and true. It was her visionary landscape. In Venice, having Zandra's drawings translated into cloth on a still-operational loom designed by Leonardo da Vinci gave our partnership a sacral aura.

Meeting Zandra, to me, meant facing the beauty of revolutionary artists. She is incredibly strong and kind at the same time, and she is a good friend, and I love her. Grazie Zandra, for being who you are.

Rhodes's rendition of Hieronymus Bosch's *The Garden of Early Delights* (1490–1500) for the Valentino Spring/Summer 2017 collection.

left to right

Close-up of Rhodes's rendition of *The Garden of Early Delights*
on a Valentino gown.
Close-up of Rhodes's 'Love Blade' beaded on a Valentino gown.
Close-up of Rhodes's rendition of *The Garden of Early Delights*
on a Valentino gown.
Courtesy of Valentino SpA. Photos by Greg Kessler.

top row to bottom row, from left to right

Portraits of Zandra Rhodes from various collections by Robyn Beeche.
S/S 1975/76 'Cactus and Cowboy' collection; S/S 1980 'Chinese'
collection; S/S 1981 'African' collection; S/S 1985 'Images of Woman'
collection; A/W 1982 'The Indian' collection; S/S 1986 'Spanish
Impressions' collection; A/W 1983 'Medieval' collection; S/S 1987
'Secrets of the Nile' collection; S/S 1984 'Fables of the Sea' collection.

A STORY OF PUNK, PRINCESSES, PAINTINGS, PATTERNS AND PECULIAR PARALLELS

Zandra Rhodes

My mother taught dressmaking at Medway College of Design (now part of the University for Creative Arts). She would always be working; from her I learned hard, continual work and perseverance in the face of any obstacle! We didn't have a television until I was 17, so we would listen to the radio and I would sketch. I always loved painting and drawing. I never saw myself making clothes and my mother never taught me at Medway. What she did teach me was to believe in myself: she told me I could be and do anything and I believed her. When I started studying printed textiles at college in the 1950s, I had an amazing teacher, Barbara Brown, who was always wonderfully enthusiastic. From there my love of printed textiles grew. Barbara encouraged me to study at London's Royal College of Art, so I applied and won a scholarship for printed textiles.

The mid-1960s were the heyday of beautiful furnishing fabrics, produced by companies such as Hull Traders and Heal's. Designers such as Audrey Levy and Shirley Craven were dominant. However, dress fabrics in the 60s were in the doldrums. At this time, the renowned printed fabric shop Liberty was producing tiny, all-over prints that were fairly nondescript and made no statement. Meanwhile, I was still finding my way, experimenting with print design. I wanted to do something creative but hadn't yet worked out what aspect of textile design I would specialise in. Then the Italian fashion designer Emilio Pucci happened in Italy! Suddenly, I wanted to make designs with patterns that made a statement and were created specially for wearing. Not curtains; something conceived to be worn around a body, not a window! Since fashion was in my blood through my mother, I guess it was a given that one day I would apply my 'art' to clothing.

When designing textiles, I would hold the paper design up against me and look in the mirror so that I could follow the layout of the print and see the exact size and placement on the body. I would think of what the pattern would do, how it would look as a dress, how it would drape and what sort of shape it would make. For me, the printed textile pattern is the essential component; it is not something that can be idly cut up and carelessly destroyed (something I feel many dress designers are guilty of doing). I wanted my garments to be controlled by the print. It was because of the print that each particular garment came into being. If the print was based on a shawl, it became a shawl-type jacket – I cut around the pattern exactly as the print dictated: this is how the 'Chevron Shawl' jacket happened (see pp. 24–25).

My first solo collection was presented in 1969. For this collection, I used three different fabrics: printed felt, printed satin and printed silk chiffon. These three fabrics made up my first collection and somehow caught the public's attention, and notably that of the high priestess of American *Vogue*, Diana Vreeland, and, in the UK, that of a young editor, Marit Allen, who took me to see Beatrix Miller, the editor-in-chief of British *Vogue*. Both of these strong editors featured my clothes. Diana Vreeland had them photographed on Natalie Wood (see pp. 21–22) and started introducing me to key New York society ladies, as well as the vibrant 54th Street boutique store Henri Bendel. This was my launch in the United States. From this first visit on, I started to travel to America to show my collections twice a year.

During the early 1970s, I founded a fabulous, chic boutique with Ronnie Stirling and Anne Knight, designed by Richard Holley, and additional boutiques in the department stores Bloomingdale's, New York and Marshall Field's, Chicago. My London boutique was in Mayfair just off the middle of Bond Street. It became the go-to shop in fashionable London and was so well known that when we had a robbery – in which the robbers somehow extricated my fantasy dresses through the mail box – it made headlines everywhere, and even a cartoon by JAK in the *Evening Standard*! It was into this shop that the young Diana Spencer came with her friend Sarah Ferguson. Later, when I was working on the 2005 exhibition *Zandra Rhodes: A Lifelong Love Affair with Textiles* at the Fashion and Textile Museum in London, Christian Lacroix wrote how, as a student, he used to come to London and gaze into my shop windows.

I also started doing my fantasy fashion shows at this time. When it came to my very first London dress show, I wanted this to be an amazing experience – something that had never been done before. One unique touch was inspired by Michael Chow, one of my early mentors (I had developed a friendship with him after dining at his famous restaurant with my dear friend and fabulous hairdresser, Leonard). On Michael's advice, I created a signed and numbered poster for the show, which took place at the Roundhouse in London in 1972. This first poster used a photograph of Anjelica Houston by Clive Arrowsmith; Anjelica had her make-up done by Barbara Daly and her hair by Leonard. The show was electric! An ultimate fantasy moment and still remembered by many as their great London experience – for example, Australian clothing designer Jenny Kee, here reminiscing in her book *A Big Life*:

> [Zandra's] 'I Love Lilies' theme had its debut at the Roundhouse [t]heatre towards the end of 1972. It was the highlight event of my London fashion experience. The parade, choreographed to Rio Carnivale [*sic*] music, opened with models wearing pearl-encrusted masks created by the legendary make-up artist Barbara Daly. Mick Milligan made enormous gold-foil lilies set on tremblers for head and throat.
>
> The models, who included Renate Zatch [*sic*], Caterine Milinaire, Anjelica Huston, Warhol superstar Donna Jordan, Orson Welles's daughter, Beatrice, and the Ethiopian model Selina, wore quilted, printed and flowing chiffon kaftans and exotic ruched and smocked jerseys with exposed reversed seams. The bride (Cathee Dahmen) was dressed in heavy guipure lace, with frills and a trumpet skirt cut to resemble an inverted lily.
>
> I was transfixed. Zandra's work was dramatic, graceful,

rich with history yet absolutely original. I decided, then and there, that this woman was a genius.[1]

There were many other memorable shows in the 1970s. The interior designer Maxine Smith, now a dear friend, not only hunted me out and began to collect my clothes from the days of my Bayswater attic studio, but also brought them to Los Angeles, to Charles Gallay's shop on Camden Drive and the film-star world. Together with her husband Gary, producer and director at ATV, she thought I should take the 'Midnight' show to New York. Gary introduced me to the owner of the Circle in the Square Theatre. It was here that I staged my show in 1974 with 'Little Nell' Campbell (of *The Rocky Horror Picture Show*) and Beatrice Welles (daughter of Orson Welles) as my models. In 1976, I had another showing at the Roundhouse, this one featuring my 'Cactus and Cowboy' collection – this was before any American designers considered this theme! In this show I created chiffon corrals and the models danced around the stage in cowboy boots and printed ultrasuede dresses, jackets and trousers.

Some time in the late 1970s, the group who ran the large Olympia exhibition centre called me and asked me to see a hall in the complex that had been closed and not used for many years. They did not know what to do with it. When I saw it my jaw dropped! It was a hidden, secret, cobwebbed room. I called it the 'Magnificent Pillar Hall'. It was here, throughout the 1980s, that I created my most memorable shows. Before that time, apart from the Roundhouse, I had used the Savoy Hotel and the King's Road Theatre, home of *The Rocky Horror Show*, where, in one show, my bride started from the back of the auditorium and her veil gradually floated down from the balcony as she moved forward, ending up running the length of the theatre. My shows became the ultimate fashion experience of fashion week, and people would travel from all over the world to London to come and see them.

In the late 1970s I had sensed a change coming; I felt it in my bones! I was inspired by street punk to create the 'Conceptual Chic' collections of 1977/78 (the phrase coined by the painter and pioneer of the Maximalist movement, my close friend Duggie Fields). This was my revolutionary jersey collection with holes, bejewelled safety pins and chains, on fine French Racine jersey material in black and pink – no print! The inspiration came from the streets, not high fashion. Other notable shows included my Egyptian show, 'Secrets of the Nile' (1987), where the girls were made to walk sideways and backwards in poses as if they were hieroglyphics. For the 'Spanish Impressions' collection of a year earlier, Ben Scholton and myself worked all night on choosing amazing Spanish music with castanets. Phyllis Cohen designed incredible stick-on eye patches and my models transformed into performers!

I have had most of my best inspiration through travel, especially with my close friend Andrew Logan. We have had fabulous adventures together: India, China, Morocco and more. We get up, have breakfast, walk around and draw something – at least one

top to bottom
Photograph of Rhodes's mother, Beatrice.
Rhodes's shop on Grafton Street, London, designed by Richard Holley.
'It's a little number I had nicked in London!' – *Evening Standard* cartoon after a robbery at Rhodes's Grafton Street shop, 10 April 1985.

1   Jenny Kee with Samantha Trenoweth, *A Big Life*, Camberwell, Vic.: Lantern, 2006, p. 121.

drawing or watercolour a day, maybe two or three. When we're done, maybe we'd go to a museum, or if we were really tired, we'd go shopping! My prints and the themes of my collections nearly always come from trips, when I'm lucky enough to get away. One of the most lasting and inspirational journeys I have had so far started in 1981, when I was invited to India by the Handicraft & Handlooms Exports Corporation (HHEC), headed by an amazing lady, Pupul Jayakar. I was taken around India by the inspirational Rajeev Sethi, now a close friend – colour! Colour! Colour! This has led to so many new adventures. My first Indian show was in Fall 1982; fantastic blue make-up by Yvonne Gold and coloured plaits bought from Indian markets on all the models. Another of my shows, 'India Revisited', used wonderful music by Ananda Shankar called 'Dancing Peacocks', which I discovered in a record shop in Bombay. Through my visits to India I started to get my patterns interpreted in zari beadwork to create all-over beaded dresses, dramatically enhancing my exotic patterns three-dimensionally.

One of my most notable American shows was for Martha's boutique in New York, and took place at the Pierre Hotel, choreographed by Ron Link and filmed by Andy Warhol. Imagine my surprise when I went to the Andy Warhol Museum in Pittsburgh many years later – I was overseeing my designs for Georges Bizet's *The Pearl Fishers* at Pittsburgh Opera – and saw my Martha's New York fashion show playing in all its glory in the gallery! Another of my shows in the United States, also choreographed by Ron Link, was for the Contemporary Art Museum in La Jolla, California (now the Museum of Contemporary Art San Diego). That was in May of 1982 and those who attended still remember it today as the pinnacle of their fashion show experience!

All through the 1970s, 80s and early 90s I celebrated my different shows with signed and numbered posters: art posters featuring fabulous stars such as Marisa Berenson and Anjelica Houston, made with the top photographers Clive Arrowsmith, Barry Lategan and, later, Robyn Beeche. For these images, I worked with some of the most amazing, brilliant, avant-garde make-up artists: Barbara Daly, Richard Sharah, Phyllis Cohen and Yvonne Gold, and hairdressers Leonard and Trevor Sorbie. We were 25 years ahead of our time. Together, we captured my essential look for each season, which I also embodied by dyeing my hair in bright colours, later becoming the poster model. I myself have always dressed to follow the look that I promote each season – from green hair to hand-drawn lipstick curls on my face. On meeting Angelo Donghia of Vice Versa in 1969, he commented that 'If you look like that, your work must be marvellous.' Those posters are now collector's items.

In the mid-1990s, I met Salah Hassanein, who was to become my lifetime partner. I started to travel the world with him, which happily coincided with my US shows and licensing work in Japan (where he was busy building multiplex cinemas for Warner Brothers). Around 1993, Salah retired from all this travel to become president of the post-production company Todd-AO and decided he wanted to live

top to bottom
Princess Diana wearing a white Zandra Rhodes gown to a charity gala in aid of Birthright at the London Palladium in June 1987. Photo: Jayne Fincher.
David Sassoon and Zandra Rhodes at the opening of the Barbican Centre in 1982. Photo courtesy of David Sassoon.
Andrew Logan and Zandra Rhodes posing backstage at one of Rhodes's fashion shows in the 1980s.

with me by the sea in Del Mar, California and commute to Los Angeles for work. Salah agreed that I should split my life between California and London, keeping my design company in London, with a satellite studio and life with him in California. At this time, my factory in Hammersmith was run by Ben Scholton (who had been with me first as a student since 1972, then later became co-designer/co-manager with me). I had a beautiful house in St Stephen's Gardens, Notting Hill, as well as a studio in Bayswater at the back of Paddington station. I continued to show around the United States with Neiman Marcus, Saks and Martha's, and came back and forth to and from London for fashion weeks and to work on the collections. I had, however, closed my Mayfair shop and concession in Harrods, separated from my partners and reduced my production.

In fashion the only constant is change.[2] I think that the fashion industry in the twenty-first century, in particular, is a more difficult, cut-throat world. Champagne and handbags and perfume keep companies going; many fashion companies are not supported by the clothes. I had embarked on several perfume projects, but these had not materialised into a brand or empire. It seemed that the world had forgotten me and was semi-ignoring my work, so I began to broaden my horizons. But first, disaster struck. I had always tried to keep my key designs, rather than selling them. Most of my favourite original samples were stored in giant silver trunks in a west London storage unit. Even though I felt as if the world was ignoring me then, I was convinced that I should preserve my work and that they would not ignore me in the end (whenever that end might be!). Then, during Christmas of 1995, my storage unit got flooded so that boxes of irreplaceable sample garments got soaked with water. The storage unit manager called my London studio, but I was away in California and the staff were all away on holiday! I immediately flew back to London and called Frances Diplock. Frances had run my hand-finishing workroom and would travel over to India for two weeks to oversee each season and the sampling when I was doing my Indian beaded dresses, but at this time she had retired. She came back in the middle of winter, together with her thermos flask, and we dried and repacked my precious dresses. Additionally, at this time my silk screens were also stored all over London because I had reduced the printing space in the Shepherd's Bush factory in order to rent out part of the building. My printing was now once again being done in my old studio in Bayswater, where I had started!

At this time my problems seemed insurmountable. Then, coincidentally, Andrew Logan, who had his magical glass-house studio in Bermondsey, rang me up and said 'There is a large warehouse up for sale near me and you've always wanted to create a museum.' My automatic reply was 'Do you think I'm made of money?' Nevertheless, he and his partner, Michael Davis, showed me the building in dilapidated, forgotten Bermondsey Street. There were no shops open – many of the buildings had been boarded up since the wartime bombings and the Shard had not yet been built!

2   A version of this comment appeared in Alison Beard,
'Life's Work: An Interview with Zandra Rhodes', *Harvard
Business Review*, April 2014, https://hbr.org/2014/04/zandra-
rhodes (accessed February 2019).

Even though it seemed a bit mad considering the circumstances, I couldn't get the idea of this wonderful building out of my head. Things began to gel! This warehouse could be the perfect answer: I could consolidate my storage (which was spread all over London); there was a long room on the side of the building – a perfect space for my print room and a studio space for textile design and manufacture; and I could also live on site and have space for the museum! The idea was born: I would sell my Notting Hill home to buy the building, then I would sell my other buildings, including the Bayswater studio and factory. Together with Michael Davis, I carefully chose top Mexican architect Ricardo Legorreta to design the building for me. I then procured a special personal introduction to Ricardo, as my partner Salah had friends whose house he had designed. This was to be his first building in Europe!

The Fashion and Textile Museum was opened in 2003 by Princess Michael of Kent, who is its patron. This connection was brought about by my great friend and mentor David Sassoon (of Bellville Sassoon). David is one of the greats of English fashion, to whom I talk daily. He has been my close friend for so many adventures – always able to pinpoint the direction in which I should head. It was David who encouraged me to do my fantasy crinolines of the 1970s and it was he who wrote and asked Princess Michael to be our patron and to open the museum. So I had managed to move, found a museum, and consolidate my buildings, workrooms and storage. My next challenge was to expand my horizons to the world of opera!

During this period, when I felt that my dresses were being ignored by the mainstream industry, I had been creating another life and clientele in San Diego with Salah, and this is where I met the general director of the San Diego Opera, Ian Campbell. He asked me, 'Why have you never done an opera?' I said, 'I've never been asked! Zeffirelli once called me but he never rang back!' Ian then proposed that I design costumes for *The Magic Flute* (2001, see pp. 149–150). Following that, I was commissioned to design sets and costumes for Georges Bizet's *The Pearl Fishers* (2004, see p. 151). Then Anthony Freud at the Houston Opera asked me to design the costumes and sets for *Aida* (2007, see pp. 152–54).

Then John Galliano started showing flowy chiffon in his collections in Paris in the early 2000s, a fabric that had been ignored for many years. The world looked again to Zandra Rhodes fantasy chiffons, and my work was back in the spotlight! My print room was now in operation once more and my fantasy prints were being rediscovered. I looked to my classic styles and produced two 'Archive' collections, bringing out editions of some of my most valued original print designs.

In summer 2016, Pierpaolo Piccioli, creative director of Maison Valentino, approached me to collaborate with him on a collection of prints for his first solo collection (Spring/Summer 2017), and then again for the Resort 2018 collection. Pierpaolo and the Valentino team came to London to see work from my archives. Working with Pierpaolo was as much a pleasure as it was an honour. The way his mind re-mastered my prints and designs from so long ago was extraordinary. Watching these designs drift by me in Paris moved me; I loved to see my original prints reborn in such a beautiful way.

This book endeavours to provide a pictorial history of my key garments and prints from the past 50 years, taking you, the reader, on a journey through my main love – printed textile designs. I hope that these pages reveal the amazing adventures on which they've taken me: fabulous flowing silk chiffons, hand rolled and edged with pearls; printed, quilted, pleated satins; printed ultrasuede; zari beadwork; discharge-printed velvet and satin devoré velvet; and hand-painted chiffon and bleached denim. Above all, it expresses my love for what prints and fabrics can be made into and how they can be worn.

As a designer, it is your work that you can stand or fall by. I have stuck to my beliefs and been true to myself and my art. However, I have always felt like I am a tightrope walker who could fall at any time, because the terrain of fashion is perpetually turbulent. I am always happily laid bare in my print design; it comes from my eyes, to my mind, to my hand – there's a higher channelling process for anyone who comes up with an original idea. Sometimes the flow comes so easily; sometimes not so. We are thankfully now in a time that is focusing again on process. As you get older, you're worried you won't be able to keep up with the status quo. You hope that the system hasn't beaten you down and that you do keep coming up with radical ideas. The trouble is that the more well known you are, the more difficult it is to hide away to work. When no one's interested in you or inviting you to things, it's easier.

No matter what I do now, the fact that my early works are in the Victoria and Albert Museum, London and New York's Metropolitan Museum of Art is all anyone could want from a career. Most of all, I'd like to be remembered for my creations in the field of textile design and for doing things differently. I was honoured to be made Dame Commander of the Order of the British Empire in the Queen's Honours list of 2014, presented to be by Anne, Princess Royal – a highlight of my career that made me feel I had really made an impact.

If I had any advice to those starting out in the world of fashion, it would be to keep going by whatever means you can. Don't let people crush you. Have an inner belief in yourself. In the end, what you do will come through. We suffer today from people wanting fame rather than earning fame through their work. Your work is what you're here for, and you should do it regardless. If it brings you something else, that's a plus. You can be ambitious, but you have to be content with the fact that it might not make you a millionaire. It's always the original thought that sells best.

Work harder than you think you can, find your tribe, be kind, say yes, and help others wherever possible.[3]

3   A version of this comment appeared in Lara Monro, 'Interview with Zandra Rhodes', Marguerite London, http://margueritelondon.com/zandra-rhodes (accessed February 2019).

LIST OF COLLECTIONS

1969: 'Knitted Circle' collection
Spring/Summer 1970: 'Ukraine and Chevron Shawl' collection
Autumn/Winter 1970: 'New York and Indian Feathers' collection
Spring/Summer 1971: 'Elizabethan Slashed Silk' collection
Autumn/Winter 1971: 'Paris, Frills and Button Flowers' collection
Autumn/Winter 1972: 'The Lily' collection
Autumn/Winter 1973: 'The Shell' collection at the Savoy
Autumn/Winter 1974: 'Ayers Rock' collection
Spring/Summer 1976: 'Cactus and Cowboy' collection at the Roundhouse
Autumn/Winter 1976–78: 'Mexican' collections
Spring/Summer 1977/78: 'Conceptual Chic' collections
Autumn/Winter 1978: 'Painted Lady' collection
Autumn/Winter 1979: 'Magic Head' collection
Spring/Summer 1980: 'Chinese' collection
Autumn/Winter 1980: 'Chinese Constructive' collection
Spring/Summer 1981: 'African' collection
Autumn/Winter 1981: 'Renaissance/Gold' collection
Spring/Summer 1982: 'Fairy' collection
Autumn/Winter 1982: 'The Indian' collection
Spring/Summer 1983: 'Mount Olympus' collection
Autumn/Winter 1983: 'Medieval' collection
Spring/Summer 1984: 'Fables of the Sea' collection
Autumn/Winter 1984: 'Magic Carpet' collection
Spring/Summer 1985: 'Images of Woman' collection
Autumn/Winter 1985: 'India Revisited' collection
Spring/Summer 1986: 'Spanish Impressions' collection
Autumn/Winter 1986: 'Ode to Woman' collection
Spring/Summer 1987: 'Secrets of the Nile' collection
Autumn/Winter 1987: 'Wish Upon a Star' collection
December 1987: 'Indian Sari' collection in Bombay and Delhi
Spring/Summer 1988: 'Fantastic Flower Garden' collection
Autumn/Winter 1988: 'Elements of Woman' collection
Spring/Summer 1989: 'Venetian Splendour' collection
Autumn/Winter 1989: 'Queen of Hearts' collection
Spring/Summer 1990: 'Zandra Goes to Hollywood' collection
Autumn/Winter 1990: 'Temples and Lotuses' collection
Spring/Summer 1991: 'Flower Power' collection
Autumn/Winter 1991: 'Celestial Bodies' collection
Spring/Summer 1992: 'Cinderella Dreams in Colour' collection
Autumn/Winter 1992: 'Pretty Woman' collection
Spring/Summer 1993: 'The Classics' collection
Autumn/Winter 1993: 'Neo-Fantasy Look' collection
Spring/Summer 1994: 'Quiet Luxury' collection
Autumn/Winter 1994: 'Divine Diva' collection
Spring/Summer 1995: 'Rocco English Rhodes Garden' collection
Autumn/Winter 1995: 'An Unfinished Symphony' collection
Spring/Summer 1996: 'Cretian Splendour' collection
Autumn/Winter 1996: 'ZR II and White Rose' collection

Autumn/Winter 1998: 'Exclusive to Liberty' collection
Spring/Summer 1999: 'Luxurious Satin and Velvet' collection
Autumn/Winter 1999: 'Floral Explosion' collection
Spring/Summer 2000: 'Seashell Fantasy' collection
Autumn/Winter 2000: 'Lipstick and Leaves' collection
Spring/Summer 2001: 'The Magic Flute' collection
Autumn/Winter 2001: 'Graffiti' collection
Spring/Summer 2002: 'Ethereal Inspiration' collection
Autumn/Winter 2002: 'Desert Queen' collection
Spring/Summer 2003: 'Birds of Paradise' collection
Autumn/Winter 2003: 'Field of Lilies' collection
Spring/Summer 2004: 'Pop' collection
Autumn/Winter 2004: 'Patterns Everywhere' collection
Spring/Summer 2005: 'Thoughts about Aida' collection
Autumn/Winter 2005: 'Flowers, Flounces and Frills' collection
Spring/Summer 2006: 'Peasant Roses' collection
Autumn/Winter 2006: 'Lacy Body Landscapes' collection
Spring/Summer 2007: 'House of Zandra' collection
Autumn/Winter 2007: 'Looping the Loops' collection
Spring/Summer 2008: 'Sparkling Sequin' collection
Autumn/Winter 2008: 'Rose Shawl and Mondrian' collection
Spring/Summer 2009: 'Dandelion' collection
Autumn/Winter 2009: 'Striped Whirlwind' collection
Spring/Summer 2010: 'Stardust' collection
Autumn/Winter 2010: 'Dream Flower' collection
Spring/Summer 2011: 'Stardust Stripe' collection
Autumn/Winter 2011: 'Pearls & Pleating' collection
Spring/Summer 2012: 'Gypsy Kaleidoscope' collection
Autumn/Winter 2012: 'New Beginnings' collection
Spring/Summer 2013: 'The Sketchbook' collection
Autumn/Winter 2013: 'Fringe Follies' collection
Spring/Summer 2014: 'Jewels & Pearl Drops' collection
Autumn/Winter 2014: 'Go Red for Women' collection
Spring/Summer 2015: 'Tulip and Ribbon' collection
Autumn/Winter 2015: 'Lace Forest' collection
Spring/Summer 2016: 'Batik' collection
Autumn/Winter 2016: 'Songket Brocade' collection
Spring/Summer 2017: 'Archive Collection I'
Spring/Summer 2017: 'Valentino X Zandra Rhodes' collection
Spring/Summer 2017: 'Zandra Rhodes's Print Designs for Valentino' collection
Autumn/Winter 2017: 'Archive Collection II'
Resort 2018: 'Zandra Rhodes's Print Designs for Valentino' collection
Autumn/Winter 2018: 'Party' collection
Spring/Summer 2019: 'Looking Back, Looking Forward' collection
Autumn/Winter 2019: 'The Golden Hour' collection

ACKNOWLEDGEMENTS

A special thank you to Dakota Amber Scoppettuolo, who has worked tirelessly on this book for the last six months: researching, collecting, archiving, and selecting and editing all of the imagery and descriptions, as well as steering the project and the essay contributors.

The Fashion and Textile Museum would like to thank the following:

Iris Apfel, Marylou Luther, Helena Matheopoulos, Suzy Menkes, Pierpaolo Piccioli, Joan Agajanian Quinn, Mary Schoeser, Rajeev Sethi and Anna Sui for their contributions.

Newham College of Further Education and its board of governors and executive board for their continued support for the Fashion and Textile Museum.

Dame Zandra Rhodes and her team for founding the Museum and their continued inspiration.

Zandra Rhodes would like to thank:

Suzy Menkes, a loyal friend for whom I have great respect. I am very honoured that she has written the foreword to this book and supported my career over the years.

My great friend Joan Quinn (never without her camera), who has been able to recall so many marvellous memories and who, with her husband Jack, has been such a key part of my life in the US.

The fabulous friends and associates who contributed essays to this book: Iris Apfel, Mary Schoeser, Helena Matheopoulos, Marylou Luther, Anna Sui, Pierpaolo Piccioli and Rajeev Sethi – who is not only an inspirational friend but started me on all of my adventures in India. Thank you, too, to Dennis Nothdruft who, as curator at the Fashion and Textile Museum, is the one who sparked the idea for this book to celebrate my 50 fabulous years in fashion and its accompanying exhibition.

A huge thank you to those photographers whose work I have used to recall the wonderful key moments of my career, capturing the atmosphere of my dresses as they were happening in various editorials, or from their own personal files or in celebration posters: Barry Lategan, David Bailey and Clive Arrowsmith, then Robyn Beeche, without whom this book could not have even happened and who set herself the task of recording all of my work during her lifetime. Thank you also to Norman Parkinson, whose photo of Princess Anne in my clothes featured on the cover of so many magazines worldwide in a strange and amazing breakthrough of fate.

In my own London studio, Frances Diplock, my anchor throughout, knows my designs better than I do: recalling, retracing and lovingly restoring my work for photography. Ben Scholton, who created collections with me for over 25 years, and Jill Griffiths, who worked with me in my Bayswater Studio on my textile collections for many years. A million thank yous to my family of supporters and fashionistas in San Diego, including Martha Gafford and Valerie Cooper, who kindly donated several of my most memorable pieces, and especially to Jeanne Jones who (in addition to having a large collection of my garments) sponsored my first opera designs for *The Magic Flute* when it made its debut at the San Diego Opera.

Thank you to my many friends and supporters of my work. David Sassoon, who has encouraged me through everything. Andrew Logan, a part of so many of my adventures, and Duggie Fields, who is the most amazing friend and sounding board. My sister Beverley, who has always been there for me. Pat O'Connor, who unhesitatingly stepped in at the 11th hour to guarantee this book happened. Marit Leiberson, who as a young editor took me to Bea Miller, and Bea for giving me the letter of introduction to Diana Vreeland of *Vogue*, who then became a prominent supporter of my work. Barbara Nessim, who draws every day and has encouraged me always to treasure all that I do and to save it and record all throughout. The loveable and private Divine (Divii) and John Waters, who entered my life when Divine passed. Ronnie Stirling for initially believing in me and backing my fabulous Mayfair shop.

Finally, I dedicate this book to Salah Hassanein, my partner for the last 30 years, who has always encouraged me and allowed me to continue my work.

Salah enabled me to create the Fashion and Textile Museum when I failed to achieve a Lottery bid, introducing me to Mexican architect Ricardo Legorreta, who did an incredible job designing the building. It was Salah who conceived partnering with Newham College of Further Education and their inspired head, Martin Tolhurst, to create not just an educational hub but also the exciting Fashion and Textile Museum.

BIBLIOGRAPHY

Adamson, Glenn, Jane Pavitt and Paola Antonelli. *Postmodernism: Style and Subversion, 1970–1990*. London: V&A Publishing, 2011.

Baxter-Wright, Emma. *Vintage Fashion: Collecting and Wearing Designer Classics*. London: Carlton Books, 2015. Foreword by Zandra Rhodes.

Cawthorne, Nigel, Emily Evans, Marc Kitchen-Smith, Kate Mulvey and Melissa Richards. *Key Moments in Fashion: The Evolution of Style*. London: Hamlyn, 2001.

Dresses from the Collection of Diana, Princess of Wales. New York: Christie's, 1997.

Eastoe, Jane and Sarah Gristwood. *Fabulous Frocks*. London: Pavilion Books, 2013.

Ehrman, Edwina. *The Wedding Dress: 300 Years of Bridal Fashions*. London: V&A Publishing, 2014.

Fogg, Marnie, ed. *Fashion: The Whole Story*. London: Thames and Hudson, 2013.

Graham, Tim and Tamsin Blanchard. *Dressing Diana*. London: Weidenfeld and Nicolson, 1998.

Grumbach, Didier. *History of International Fashion*. Northampton, MA: Interlink Books, 2014.

Jackson, Laura. *Freddie Mercury: The Biography*. London: Piatkus, 2012.

Jackson, Lesley. *20th Century Pattern Design: Textile & Wallpaper Pioneers*. London: Mitchell Beazley, 2011.

Kee, Jenny and Samantha Trenoweth. *A Big Life*. Camberwell, Victoria: Lantern, 2006.

Keenan, Brigid. *The Women We Wanted to Look Like*. London: Macmillan, 1978.

Knight, Anne and Zandra Rhodes. *The Art of Zandra Rhodes*. London: Jonathan Cape, 1984.

Lutyens, Dominic and Kirsty Hislop. *70s Style and Design*. London: Thames and Hudson, 2009.

Matheopoulos, Helena. *Fashion Designers at the Opera*. New York: Thames and Hudson, 2011.

Monsef, Gity, Dennis Nothdruft and Robert de Niet. *Zandra Rhodes: A Lifelong Love Affair with Textiles*. Woodbridge, Suffolk: Antique Collectors' Club, 2005.

Monsef, Gity, Samantha Erin Safer and Robert de Niet. *My Favourite Dress*. Woodbridge, Suffolk: Antique Collectors' Club, 2010. Afterword by Zandra Rhodes.

Rayner, Geoffrey, Richard Chamberlain and Annamarie Stapleton. *Pop!: Design, Culture, Fashion, 1956–1976*. Woodbridge, Suffolk: ACC Editions, 2012.

Safer, Samantha Erin. *Zandra Rhodes – Textile Revolution: Medals, Wiggles and Pop 1961–1971*. Woodbridge, Suffolk: Antique Collectors' Club, 2010.

Schoeser, Mary. *Textiles: The Art of Mankind*. London: Thames and Hudson, 2012.

Steele, Valerie. *Women of Fashion: Twentieth Century Designers*. New York: Rizzoli, 1991.

Tolkien, Tracy. *Vintage: The Art of Dressing Up*. London: Pavilion Books, 2002.

York, Peter. *Style Wars*. London: Sidgwick and Jackson, 1980.

PICTURE CREDITS

Evening Standard LTD. 2018: p. 200 (bottom)

Personal files of Zandra Rhodes: pp. 10 (all), 11 (all), 12 (all), 16, 60 (bottom right), 92, 122 (left), 124 (all), 125 (right), 146, 149 (bottom), 150 (bottom), 151 (top and middle), 154 (top), 172 (middle and bottom), 173 (top), 194, 200 (top and middle), 201 (bottom)

Photo by Alexis Duclos / Gamma-Rapho / Getty Images: p. 52 (top right)

Photo by Andrew Woffinden: pp. 186, 189

Photo by Art Kane ©: p. 60 (top left and top right)

Photo by Barry Lategan / Vogue © The Condé Nast Publications Ltd: pp. 38–39

Photo by Barry Lategan: p. 43

Photo by Bill Cunningham / Courtesy of Anna Sui: p. 61 (bottom)

Photo by Bill King / Harper's Bazaar © Hearst: p. 59 (bottom)

Photo by Bishin Jumonji: p. 33

Photo by Bridie O'Sullivan: p. 177

Photo by Charles Tracy / Vogue © The Condé Nast Publications Ltd: p. 54

Photo by Christopher Bissell: pp. 109, 134

Photo by Clive Arrowsmith / Vogue © The Condé Nast Publications Ltd: pp. 30, 59 (top), 148

Photo by Clive Arrowsmith: pp. 44, 48, 49, 50, 61 (top)

Photo by Clive Boursnell: p. 56 (top and bottom)

Photo by Cory Weaver; taken at the San Francisco Opera: pp. 152–3, 154 (bottom)

Photo by Dakota Amber Scoppettuolo: p. 123 (left)

Photo by David Bailey / Vogue © The Condé Nast Publications Ltd: pp. 19, 29, 34

Photo by Dominic Lipinski: p. 202 (bottom)

Photo by Eric Bowman: p. 4

Photo by Emma Hampson-Jones and Luke Reynolds / Stylist: Kim Howells: p. 178

Photo by Eva Sereny / Iconic Images: p. 58

Photo by Francesco Scavullo: p. 13 (bottom)

Photo by Gianni Penati / Vogue © The Condé Nast Publications Ltd: pp. 21, 22

Photo by Grant Mudford: p. 46 (top left)

Photo by Greg Kessler / Courtesy of Valentino SpA: pp. 196–7

Photo by Greg Barrett: p. 127 (left)

Photo by Henry Clarke / Vogue © The Condé Nast Publications Ltd: p. 26

Photo by Jacob Lewis, The Magic Flute, courtesy of Seattle Opera: p. 150 (middle)

Photo by Jayne Fincher / Getty Images: p. 201 (top)

Photo by Jill Green: p. 139

Photo by Kelly Robinson: p. 125 (left)

Photo by Ken Goff / GoffPhotos: p. 202 (middle)

Photo by Ken Howard, courtesy of San Diego Opera: pp. 149 (top), 151 (bottom)

Photo by Maria von Matthiessen / Harper's Bazaar: p. 13 (top)

Photo by Mario Testino © / Vogue © The Condé Nast Publications Ltd: pp. 2–3

Photo by Masha Mel / Stylist: Kim Howells: p. 181 (both images)

Photo by Mick Rock © 1974, 2019: p. 55

Photo by Morgan O'Donovan: pp. 163, 164

Photo by Norman Eales: p. 41

Photo by Norman Parkinson / Iconic Images: p. 57

Photo by Patrick Anderson: p. 14 (bottom), 85 (bottom), 123 (right), 202 (top)

Photo by Patrick Demarchelier / Vogue © The Condé Nast Publications Ltd: p. 129

Photo by Richard Avedon © The Richard Avedon Foundation: pp. 63, 170

Photo by Richard Dowker / Model: Flora Miles / Stylist: Lily Bling / Hair: James Oxley and Team / Make-up: Claire Mulleady and the MAC Pro Team: p. 193

Photo by Robyn Beeche: pp. 9, 14 (top), 75 (all), 76, 83, 85 (top), 86, 89, 90, 93, 94, 97 (all), 99, 100, 103 (all), 105, 106, 112, 115, 122 (right), 127 (top right), 137, 173 (bottom), 198 (all)

Photo by Ron Galella/WireImage: p. 52 (bottom left)

Photo by Rozarii Lynch, The Magic Flute, courtesy of Seattle Opera: p. 150 (top)

Photo by Shane Bevel Photography, courtesy of the Tulsa Opera: p. 151 (middle)

Photo by Sheila Rock ©: p. 52 (top left)

Photo by Simon Emmett: p. 15

Photo by Stan Ripton: p. 72

Photo by Stan Woodward: p. 54 (bottom right)

Photo by Swapan Mukherjee: pp. 126, 127 (bottom right)

Photo by Tim Vechik: pp. 161, 182

Photo by Victor Virgile / Gamma-Rapho / Getty Images: p. 60 (bottom left)

Photo by Yu-Kuang Chou / Tatler © The Condé Nast Publications Ltd: p. 157

Photo courtesy of David Sassoon: p. 201 (middle)

Photo courtesy of Joan Agajanian Quinn: pp. 116 (all), 119 (all), 120 (all)

Photo: Student project at UCA managed by Piers Atkinson: pp. 98, 107

Photographs by Jon Stokes. Project managed by UCA and funded by JISC for Zandra Rhodes Digital Study Collection: pp. 20, 23, 24, 25, 27, 28, 31, 32, 35, 36, 37, 40, 42 (all), 45 (all), 46 (top right and bottom images), 47, 64, 65, 66, 67, 68, 69, 70, 71, 73, 74, 77, 78, 79, 80 (all), 81, 82, 84, 87, 88, 91, 95, 96, 101, 102, 104, 108, 110, 111, 113, 114, 147 (all)

Photographs by Jon Stokes. Project managed by Dakota Amber Scoppettuolo and funded by FTM: pp. 130, 131, 132, 133, 135, 136, 138, 140, 141, 142 (all), 143, 144, 145, 158, 159, 160, 162, 165, 166, 167, 168 (all), 169, 179, 180, 183 (all), 184 (all), 185, 187, 188, 190, 191, 192

Portrait by David Downton: p. 6

TODAY / REX / Shutterstock: p. 17

Zandra Rhodes / CVP Designs: p. 172 (top)

First published by Yale University Press 2019

302 Temple Street, P. O. Box 209040,
New Haven, CT 06520-9040
47 Bedford Square, London WC1B 3DP
yalebooks.com | yalebooks.co.uk

ISBN 978-0300-244304
Library of Congress Control Number: 2019939697
10 9 8 7 6 5 4 3 2 1
2023 2022 2021 2020 2019

Designed by Rita Peres Pereira
Research and content development by Dakota Amber
Scoppettuolo

Printed in China

Case image
Photograph of Zandra Rhodes by John Swannell, 1977